The Bible Says. . .

The Bible Says…

How Good Is the Good Book?

Larry R. Kalajainen

CASCADE *Books* · Eugene, Oregon

THE BIBLE SAYS. . .
How Good Is the Good Book?

Cascade Books
An Imprint of Wipf and Stock Publishers
199 W. 8th Ave., Suite 3
Eugene, OR 97401

www.wipfandstock.com

ISBN 13: 978-1-62032-406-6

Cataloging-in-Publication data:

Kalajainen, Larry R.

The Bible says . . . : how good is the good book? / Larry R. Kalajainen.

xii + 90 p. ; 23 cm. Includes bibliographical references.

ISBN 13: 978-1-62032-406-6

1. Bible—Canon. 2. Bible—Evidences, authority, etc. I. Title.

BS465 .K30 2013

Manufactured in the U.S.A.

To Carol

Contents

Preface

Books like this one often have multiple points of origin. One of mine was the reading and thinking I did while pursuing a graduate degree in New Testament and Early Christian Origins in the 1980s. At the time, new interdisciplinary approaches to the study of the Bible were beginning to flower. Insights from the social sciences, literary studies, the mood and concerns of "postmodern" thinking, and psycholinguistics, as well as the more traditional modes of historical criticism, were in vogue. People outside the guild of biblical scholars like Mary Douglas, Walter Ong, and Northrop Frye, along with those within the field of biblical studies like Wayne Meeks, Werner Kelber, and Bruce Malina, who were pushing for more cross-fertilization with other disciplines, opened my mind to think about the scriptures differently.

Another point of origin was the age-old pastoral task of trying to make sense out the Bible for my congregation, Sunday after Sunday in preaching and at other times in Bible studies, to help laypeople reclaim the Bible as a vital resource for their own spiritual growth and faithful action in the world around them. Attending to this pastoral work at the same time I was also doing doctoral-level academic study kept that study grounded. Around the same time, Westar's famous (or infamous, depending on one's perspective) "Jesus Seminar" was in full swing, and I was fortunate enough to participate personally in one of those meetings and to follow the Seminar's work through its publications thereafter, seeing both its benefits for the church as well as some of its weaknesses and questionable methods and agendas. One of Westar's great strengths was to bring biblical scholarship "out of the closet" where it had too often been relegated by church leaders and pastors who were afraid that learning or allowing their congregations to learn too much about the Bible would destroy their parishioners' faith or their own. My own conviction has always been that all truth is God's truth, and that whatever is true can never destroy anything, except perhaps some idolatrous illusions. I welcomed this "coming out" of the solid work of biblical scholarship of the past two centuries into the setting of the local congregation where the real work of listening for the Word of God takes place.

Because of this pastoral concern, I have deliberately tried to make the book as user-friendly as possible. My thought has been to provide busy pastors and thoughtful laypeople a way to think seriously about the Bible without getting overly bogged down in the technical scholarship regarding the biblical texts. While I have depended heavily on that scholarship, as well as my own research, most of what is said here about the Bible is information that has become general knowledge in scholarly circles, even though little of it has, until the past decade or two, crossed the invisible, but real, barriers between the academy and the pulpit or pew. Accordingly, I have tried to keep footnotes to a minimum, and to write in a style accessible to the thoughtful reader who may wish to have a layman's grasp of scholarly thinking, but who lack all the tools to do so. For the most part, I have reserved footnotes for direct citations of particular works and for extended comments for those interested.

A third originating impulse was the exhilarating and exhausting opportunity given me to become Senior Pastor of the American Church in Paris for nearly a decade following completion of my graduate work. There, in a setting where I had to preach to 500 to 700 people per week (not always the same people each week) who hailed from more than forty countries of origin and represented as many denominational or religious traditions, I discovered the power of worship structured around the church's ancient book, to bridge the chasms of culture, history, and life situations. From American corporate executives to West African refugees fleeing civil war to college students on their junior year abroad to Filipino nannies to young musicians and artists to Franco-Anglo couples, they came to hear a fresh word that would speak to them in their own particular place. It was there, in the adult church school class I taught before worship each Sunday, that this book actually began as a ten-week study. I will always be grateful to that group of twenty to thirty people who came weekly, and struggled with me through an attempt to think about the Bible in a different way. Because we brought our own religious backgrounds, beliefs, and histories with us, we entered that struggle at different points. Those who came from churches where they had been enculturated with a naïve and dogmatic literalism regarding the Bible came together with folks whose ignorance of all things biblical was vast, or who actively doubted whether anything in the Bible was either true or relevant to their lives. And, of course, there were many somewhere between those extremes who valued the Bible but just wanted some help in understanding it. That class was repeated in two subsequent congregations I've served, as well as taught to seminary students, who also received it both gratefully and critically. All these audiences contributed their own insights, and if this book has any value, it will be as much due to those communally-generated insights as to my own.

As is often the case, I am blessed with a spouse who has not only been my cherished life companion, but also my best and most patient critic. The best critics are those who offer their criticism *before* the sermon or manuscript goes public. Though not formally trained in theological or biblical criticism, she has patiently endured my need to hear myself articulating an idea before I can really know if it's what I think or not. If there are faults in my thinking and in this book, and I have no doubt that there are multiple sins of commission and omission, they are not hers.

Finally, I wish to acknowledge my debt to one of my most memorable teachers, Dr. Paul Minear. Even though I only had the privilege of studying with him for one semester, he had some of the most seminal insights into the scriptures I had ever encountered, as well as the great gift of encouragement for his students to think their own thoughts. He modeled for me the kind of scholarship that begins from a position of "standing under" the scriptures.

Soli Deo Gloria.

Larry Kalajainen
New York, July 2012

Chapter 1

Claims And Counter-Claims

"The archbishop of Canterbury has found it advisable. . ."

"Found what?" said the duck.

"Found it," replied the mouse rather crossly. "Surely you know what it means."

"Of course I know what it means when I find a thing," said the duck. "Generally, it's a frog or a worm. The question is, what did the archbishop find?"

—Lewis Carroll, *Through the Looking Glass*

Defining the Problem

"The Bible says . . ."

Through much of the latter half of the twentieth century, Americans and even people in other nations grew accustomed to seeing the American evangelist Billy Graham on their televisions or at a podium in a football stadium, Bible open in his hands, the gleam of certainty in his gaze, saying those words in authoritative tones. Such assertions are not the exclusive preserve of the Reverend Graham, however. For more than 2000 years, first Jews, and later Christians, have cited the writings that we call the Bible to authorize their views about nearly every subject imaginable, from pronouncements on such large issues as war, slavery, economics, the rights of women and homosexuals to ones of somewhat lesser import such as wearing makeup, dress codes, flying in airplanes, or playing football (or undertaking any other "secular" activity) on Sunday or the Sabbath.

A moment's thought is enough to realize that many of the claims about *what* the Bible says are often starkly contradictory. For example, in the debate over slavery in the years preceding and during the American Civil War, the Bible was the court of appeal for those on both sides of the issue. Defenders of slavery were fond of appealing to a story in Genesis 9:20–27 about Noah (he of the ark) being discovered drunk and naked in his tent by his son Ham. Though the story is somewhat ambiguous (it is Ham's son Canaan who actually gets cursed rather than Ham himself), there is at least the implication of some sort of sexual offense, since "seeing his nakedness" is not an uncommon biblical euphemism for a sexual relationship. Whatever the provocation, Ham's youngest son Canaan is the one punished by a divine curse condemning him and his descendants to slavery. Since the three sons of Noah were thought, in ancient times, to be the ancestors of the various races of people in the world, the curse that Noah pronounced upon the son of Ham (the purported ancestor of the black peoples of Africa, though this is never actually stated in the text) was used as ammunition in the argument that the enslavement of Africans was therefore justified because it was divinely sanctioned by the Bible. In addition, proponents of slavery cited references to statements by Jesus in the Gospels or in the letters of Paul such as that in Ephesians 6:5, "Slaves, obey your earthly masters with fear and trembling, in singleness of heart, as you obey Christ," that appear to accept the reality of slavery.[1]

Opponents of slavery, on the other hand, were fond of citing the various passages in the Bible dealing with God's love for all peoples, and particularly those prophetic scriptures that speak of liberation of the oppressed or St. Paul's statement in Galatians 3:28, "There is no longer Jew or Greek, slave or free, there is no longer male and female; for all of you are one in Christ." Though the issues involved in the Civil War were much more complex than simply the disagreements between North and South over slavery, it would not overstate the case to say that one prominent factor, among others, was a fundamentally divergent reading of the Bible.

Competing claims about what the Bible says continue to be a source of confusion in the church and in the larger society today. While the

---

1. The question of whether Paul is the author of both Galatians and Ephesians is irrelevant here; during the pre-Civil War period, with literary and historical criticism of the Bible still a barely emerging enterprise, both sides in the arguments over slavery would have unhesitatingly accepted Paul as the author of both. Opponents appear not to have noticed or cared that their competing citations implied that Paul was blatantly contradicting himself in the two letters.

term "the Bible" most commonly refers to the scriptures which Jews and Christians hold sacred, the conflicts generated by appeals to biblical authority are much broader than the issues that are currently causing so much internal division within the Jewish or Christian religious worlds. Debate within those communities spills over into the larger societies in which they exist. The sharp differences between the ultra-orthodox Israelis and their more moderate religious or secularized compatriots on the question of who is truly a Jew, is, in a real sense, a biblical struggle. The Bible also plays no small part in the intractable political issues between Israelis and Palestinians. Will the scriptural texts (as interpreted by the ultra-orthodox) in which God promises the land of Canaan to Israel in perpetuity, continue to justify the expansion of Israeli settlements in the West Bank and the second-class status of Arabs who are Israeli citizens, or will more pragmatic approaches of realpolitik and concerns for social justice and peaceful co-existence prevail? Similarly, the "culture wars" in the United States between "conservatives" and "liberals" are fought against a background of biblical interpretations of moral issues which one group or the other advocates writing into the law of the land. The impact of "moral values" or "family values" in the last three presidential elections was a code phrase among members of the Religious Right both for their campaign against legal abortion, as well as for the issue of whether gay persons can be married. Christians on both sides of the issue have used the Bible to buttress their positions while at the same time rejecting the biblical interpretations of their opponents. At the time of this writing, the controversy over abortion has been fanned into new flame (again). Over the past decade, the world Anglican communion has been rent by the issue of whether homosexuals may be ordained or consecrated as bishops. The same issue has similarly divided other denominations. "Conservatives," many of whom come from African or Latin American cultures, opine that their North American and Western European counterparts are proclaiming a "false gospel" that allows a "malleable, liberal interpretation of scripture."[2] "Liberals" excoriate the rigidity and dogmatism of the "Bible-thumpers." The "culture wars" are also, in a real sense, "biblical" wars.

The biblical wars are wider yet: with the rise of the various Islamic fundamentalist movements, divisions are rife within Islamic nations and cultures over the place of scriptural (Qur'anic) authority in the larger

2. Dina Kraft and Laurie Goodstein, "Anglicans Face Wider Split."

society. Should religious laws (*Shar'iah*) be the only law of the land in predominantly Muslim nations or should it govern only Muslims? In nations where Islam is a minority, should mandates drawn from the Qur'an, that Muslim women must veil themselves when in public, be permitted or should the majority culture's laws take precedence? Recently France passed legislation permitting the wearing of headcoverings for religious reasons in public, but forbidding the wearing of the *niqab*, the full facial veil, since one of the core values of French society is *egalité*—full equality of all citizens that is deemed incompatible with hiding one's face. Whether suicide bombings are a legitimate way to wage jihad are divisive questions hinging on differing interpretations of the Qur'an within the Muslim world. And when those religious traditions come into contact with the non-Islamic, secular cultures of the West, the biblical wars take on yet another dimension, pitting the sacred scriptures of one religious tradition against those of another.

It is not my intention, nor is it within my capacity, to address the specifics of each of the conflicts precipitated by competing appeals to the scriptures, nor to attempt an answer to the question of *what* the Bible says about each. Rather, my intention is to concentrate on the Christian scriptures (two-thirds of which are also the scriptures of Judaism) in an attempt to understand what it means to *claim* "the Bible says. . ." When I use the term Bible, I will, unless otherwise specified, be referring to the scriptures that Jews and Christians hold sacred. I wish to make it clear that I am speaking from within the Christian tradition, and while I believe the points I wish to make about the Bible may be useful to those within other religious traditions, particularly Judaism, I must ask the forgiveness of my readers who come from other traditions for any misrepresentations that I may unwittingly make of their positions while attempting to speak a helpful word to my own religious tribe.

I will lay out the problem with the help of some examples of competing claims about three issues that are currently causing great dissension within the Christian churches and also some synagogues and mosques, not only in the West, but in other areas of the world, as well: war, the role and status of women, and homosexuality.[3] In all three examples, the speakers or authors cited make obviously contradictory claims that the Bible "says" or "teaches" something about these issues. Whether or not

3. The recent struggle within Uganda over whether capital punishment for homosexuals would become the law of the land is another cogent example of how potentially lethal biblical interpretations may be.

one agrees with the statements being made is irrelevant to the purpose of this study; rather it is the claim that the Bible "says" or "teaches" something about these issues that should be kept in focus. In each case, read the statement in the left-hand column on the issue, and then look across the page at the right-hand column to see a contradictory claim.

The Bible Says. . .	Or Does It. . .
On War:	
"St. Augustine says in a sermon on the son of the centurion [*Ep. ad Marcel.* cxxxviii]: 'If the Christian Religion forbade war altogether, those who sought salutary advice in the Gospel would rather have been counseled to cast aside their arms, and to give up soldiering altogether. On the contrary, they were told: 'Do violence to no man . . . and be content with your pay' [Lk. 3:14.] If he [Jesus] commanded them to be content with their pay, he did not forbid soldiering.' " —Thomas Aquinas, *Summa Theologica.*[A]	"I have come to the conclusion that the Bible teaches nonresistance on the part of Christians . . . The name comes from the words of Matthew 5:39, 'That ye resist not evil . . .' Nonresistance is one aspect of the biblical teaching on separation from the world. . . Paul admonishes [the Christian] to 'be not conformed to this world' (Rom. 12:2). This includes the use of force in times of peace and also in times of war." —Herman A. Hoyt, *War: Four Christian Views.*[B]
On Homosexuality:	
"Homosexual practice is nowhere recognized in Scripture. It is condemned in both Old and New Testaments as an immoral act, and therefore a sin." —Eustace Kamanyire, Bishop of Ruwenzori in Uganda, speaking at 1998 Lambeth Conference of Anglican bishops[C]	"There are around 3000 verses in the Bible that express God's concern for the poor and oppressed. In contrast, there is a tiny handful of verses that some people claim condemn homosexuality. None of them, properly interpreted, refers to contemporary Christian people who are homosexual." —Jack Rogers, formerly Moderator of General Assembly, Presbyterian Church in the USA.[E]

A. Thomas Aquinas, *Summa Theologica*, II-II, 40.
B. Herman A. Hoyt, *War: Four Christian Views*, 31–32.
C. Amarillo Globe-News: "Anglican bishops condemn homosexual relations."
D. Robert Gagnon, "Why a New Translation."

On the Relevance of 1 Corinthians 11:2-16:	
"If inappropriate hairstyles or head coverings were a source of shame because they compromised the sexual differences of men and women, how much more would a man taking another man to bed be a shameful act, lying with another male 'as though lying with a woman'? Paul did not make head coverings an issue vital for inclusion in God's kingdom, but he did put same-sex intercourse on that level."	"Thus the Bible has relatively little to say that directly informs us about how to address the issue of homosexual Christians today. The Bible certainly does not positively condone homosexuality as a legitimate expression of human sexuality, but neither does it expressly exclude loving monogamous homosexual adult Christian relationships from being within the realm of God's intentions for humanity.
—Robert Gagnon, Associate Professor of New Testament, Pittsburgh Theological Seminary[D]	—Jeffrey Siker, Professor and Chair, Department of Theological Studies, Loyola Marymount University.[F]
On the Role of Women in Marriage:	
A wife is to submit herself graciously to the servant leadership of her husband even as the church willingly submits to the headship of Christ. (Cf. Ephesians 5:22–23)	"The concepts of headship and submission in regard to husbands and wives come together only in *Ephesians* 5:23–24. The general principle (5:21) is that all Christians should submit to each other (not all women to all men). . . 'Head' as used metaphorically in the New Testament, points overwhelmingly, *not* to a corporate organizational chart, but to a dynamic, organic, living unity—a one-flesh relationship, if you will. . . the 'head' of this living growing organism is not its ruler but the source of its life."
— official statement adopted by the Southern Baptist Convention, June 1998[G]	
"As a woman standing under the authority of scripture, even when it comes to submitting to my husband when I know he's wrong, I just have to do it."	
—Dorothy Patterson, wife of former Southern Baptist Convention president, Paige Patterson, responding to a reporter's question about the above official statement[H]	— Letha Scanzoni and Nancy Hardesty, early pioneers in biblical feminism, leaders in the Evangelical and Ecumenical Women's Caucus.[I]

E. Jack Rogers, *Jesus, the Bible, and Homosexuality*, 89.

F. Jeffrey Siker, "Homosexuality, the Bible, and Gentile Inclusion, 234.

G. Larry B. Stammer, "A Wife's Role Is 'to Submit,' Baptists Declare," online: http://articles.latimes.com/1998/jun/10/news/mn-58510.

H. John W. Kennedy, "Patterson's Election Seals Conservative Control."

I. Letha Scanzoni and Nancy Hardesty, *All We're Meant to Be*, 31.

Say, what? Or rather, says what? What does the Bible say? Can it say two contradictory things at once? Are the speakers quoted above simply misunderstanding what the Bible says? Or have they already made up their minds on the subjects at issue and are then trying to force the Bible to support their views? We know that texts can be interpreted differently, even biblical texts, but who decides which interpretation is the correct one? Is there one correct interpretation, or are all interpretations valid? Are some more valid than others?

Why appeal to the Bible at all? What is the Bible that it should be the court of appeal for particular points of view on these and other public issues? Why should people who are not practicing Jews or Christians pay any attention to the Bible at all? This is confusing! Small wonder that so few Christians, let alone those who do not profess the Christian faith, know what to think, or that the church is so divided and the debates so rancorous over these and other issues confronting our societies today. Many Christians want to claim the authority of the Bible for their views, but what can that mean when that claim is used to support diametrically opposing views of the same subject? We may be forgiven if we think that all the claims about what may be found in the Bible remind us of Lewis Carroll's inspired bit of nonsense in the epigraph to this chapter, where the archbishop is finding *it*, whatever *it* is. Our sympathies may very well lie with the duck, who just wants some straight answers.

Reiterating what I said above, it is not the purpose of this study to attempt to answer the question, "What does the Bible say about . . .?" Nor do I intend to argue for my position on the issues of war or homosexuality or the status of women, all of which are "hot-button" issues within religious communities, and in the larger society as well, though I hope that we may gain some facility in learning how to think about those questions. Rather, it is the purpose of this study to examine the claim that the Bible says or teaches something about these issues and to offer ways to think about the Bible—what it is, how it functions as an authority, how that authority is managed (or not) and by whom, and to what end. To fulfill that purpose, it will be necessary to explore how the Bible came to be.

We will look at its contents and the events and worldviews out of which the writings emerged, how these writings have been viewed, interpreted, and used down through the centuries of Jewish and Christian history, and how the Bible continues to shape the life of the religious communities that hold it sacred. I hope that by the end of this study we will all be more biblically literate, but also more capable of making discerning judgments about just what it is the Bible says, and more importantly, how the Bible may be used so that it is a life-sustaining force within the world, particularly within the faith-traditions which center around it, instead of a force that sows dissension and even incites violence as it often has and, unfortunately, still does.

Finding a Beginning Point

The issues that are claiming biblical authorization today are so fraught with emotion and divisiveness that we need to be able to step back and take a more dispassionate look at what is really going on in the use of the Bible. What do we really mean when we make the claim, "The Bible says. . ." or "The Bible teaches. . ." or when we speak of a particular viewpoint or position as "biblical?" To give us a common starting point for our discussion, I will offer five observations arising from our reading of the conflicting assertions in the table above about what the Bible says. These observations are self-evident, and each one follows logically from the one before it. While other observations undoubtedly could be made, these are important for the purposes of our study. It will be useful to state them explicitly so that we may have them in our minds when trying to think through the issues together.

- All of the speakers or authors quoted above claim, explicitly or implicitly, that the Bible says or doesn't say certain things about the three subjects: war, the role of women in home and church, and homosexuality.

- It is clear that those quoted do not agree on what the Bible says or doesn't say about these subjects.

- All of them, in some sense, recognize the Bible as an authority that undergirds their views.

- It is not clear that the words "Bible" or "scriptures" mean the same thing for all of them. All would undoubtedly agree, at the most superficial level, that the "Bible" is the collection of writings that Christians and Jews hold to be significant in some way. But it is not clear that all hold the same view of the Bible and its authority, *how* it says certain things, or what weight to give those things.

- The differences between their various understandings of "the Bible" or "the scriptures," are not merely differences in interpretation, though such differences may be immediately obvious. In other words, even if they agreed on what a given biblical passage *says* (means), they would not, in all likelihood, agree on what they or others should *do* in light of the meaning that they commonly ascribe to the text. Something more fundamental than differences in interpretation is involved in their understanding and use of the Bible.

When stated in this way, it becomes apparent that these observations raise substantive questions that will require some diligent thought in order to gain needed clarity. In the next chapter, I have identified seven of these critical questions, though there may undoubtedly be more. These will suffice for our purposes. Following each question, I've included a paragraph further expanding the question in order to illuminate its nuances or to show some of the answers that have been given both in the past and in the present.

Chapter 2

Critical Questions

If we hope to get beyond the divisiveness of competing claims, we need to be willing to examine our own and others' views about the Bible honestly without feeling threatened or defensive. While all of us have some viewpoint, and may be firmly convinced that it is the right one, it may be helpful to remember that others who hold views incompatible with ours may, nevertheless, be sincere in their quest for truth. An attitude of charity will foster an atmosphere in which real learning on all of our parts can take place. Whatever differing opinions we may hold, if we really believe that all truth is God's truth, then no sincere inquiry after that truth can ultimately lead us astray.

It is also important to remember that people in any particular religious tradition or sub-group within a tradition, use certain words or phrases that are technical jargon or "insider-speak" readily understandable by adherents or practitioners of that group, but which might not be readily intelligible to those outside it. Even among different Christian denominations or within a denomination among those who hold widely differing theological ideas, users may know what certain terms or words mean to them, but we should not assume they signify the same thing to everyone. For example, one person may speak of the Bible as "God's Word," and in her mind, may understand that phrase to refer to the actual text of the Bible, the actual words on the page. Another person may also speak of the Bible as "God's Word," but may understand that phrase as referring to the personal message or meaning of a particular biblical passage rather than to the text of the Bible itself. Another may understand it as a reference to the role that the Bible plays in the church rather than to the text or to the message of a particular passage. Such different uses of insider language can cause communication between persons to break down and misunderstandings to arise. In the questions below, I will attempt to identify with an asterisk certain phrases or terms as "insider words" that may have a range of different meanings to different people, and that would need to be clearly defined in any discussion where they are used.

1. What is the Bible?

   - Is it a single book, a divinely-inspired* special revelation* of God's will and plan? Does it all "hang together" as a coherent story which begins in Genesis and ends in the Book of Revelation? Is it an exclusively authoritative resource for all times and places? Another way to ask this aspect of the question is, "Is God the real author of the Bible?"

   - Is it a library of human writings by individuals or religious communities responding to specific events in their own times, and later recognized by other individuals or communities at a later time as containing some especially helpful insights for their own faith and life? Another way to ask this aspect of the question is, "Are human beings the real authors of the Bible?"

   - Is it a diverse collection of writings that are significant primarily because they bear witness to a faith community's (Christianity's and/or Judaism's) understanding of its relationship to God, and therefore, to be regarded as uniquely authoritative* for the community's ability to address contemporary issues? Another way to ask this question might be, "Is the Bible a community product that contains the important stories for that community's self-understanding through time?"

   - Is there significance in the order in which the books of the Bible are presented? Is this the order in which they were written? Is the order the work of early church leaders or rabbinical schools or church councils? Is this canonical* order itself divinely given, i.e., part of its inspiration*? Is it important?

   - Should the Bible be understood "literally?"* For example, is it necessary to believe that the creation of the world took place in six 24-hour periods, or that the site of the Garden of Eden may be located on a map or discovered by archaeologists? Is the book of Genesis our primary source of knowledge about the origins of the world and its inhabitants?[1] If there appears to be a difference between the modern scientific* view of the world or of historical events of the past and the accounts of those events in the Bible, must we accept the Bible's version as the true one? Is the Bible inerrant* and/or infallible* in what it affirms? What does it affirm, and how does it affirm it?

- Is the Bible primarily of historical interest as a source of information about what ancient people thought about the world and about God, but which must be demythologized* to conform to a modern scientific view of the world if it is to be of any interest or use today? In other words, does the reader of the Bible have to penetrate the "husk" of now archaic worldviews or understandings of reality in order to get at the "kernel" of spiritual truth that might be relevant for modern people?

- Is the Bible a divine oracle* (Preachers sometimes refer to the Bible as "the oracles of God") that provides an answer to every question we can think to ask about anything? Is it God's rule book for human life, so that we always know how to behave in any situation by consulting it? If we do consult it as a handbook or rule book, are there ways of consulting the Bible that are more legitimate or reliable than others? Who decides which ways are more legitimate?

- Is it a magical text with hidden meanings that can be deciphered when we uncover hidden linguistic or numerical codes with the aid of computerized analysis? This was the argument in the book *The Bible Code,*[2] that created such a furor when it was published some years ago. A similar view of the Bible as a mysteriously coded text to which only certain insiders have the key underlies the loosely-fictionalized interpretations of the Book of

---

1. Recent laws passed by the state Board of Education in Kansas and their subsequent repeal have demonstrated the impact of competing biblical interpretations of this question on the larger society. A Yankelovich poll (*International Herald Tribune,* March 13, 2000, 3) found that while 83% of Americans believe that evolution is a true explanation of how human life developed on earth, 79% also believe that creationism should be taught alongside evolution in the public schools, despite the logical inconsistency between the two positions.

2. Drosnin, *Bible Code.*

Revelation contained in the *Left Behind*[3] series of best-sellers by
Tim LaHaye and Jerry Jenkins.

All of the bulleted items above and more are answers that have been, or
are, held by various individuals and groups within Christianity and Judaism. Is one of them right? Are all the rest wrong? How do we choose? We
cannot go far in our quest to understand what claiming biblical authority
means until we come to a fundamental understanding of what the Bible
is. All the rest of the questions below are outgrowths of the primary question "What is the Bible?"

2. What role or function does (or should) the Bible play in authorizing
   the views, practices, or beliefs of the faith community or of individual believers?

   • Does (or should) it function as the ultimate authority for de-
     ciding on matters of belief, of factual truth, of behavior? Who
     gives (gave) it this role? God? Moses? The apostles? The church
     fathers? The Council of Nicea? Constantine? Anyone who reads
     it seeking God's truth? Is the answer self-evident in the Bible
     itself? Another way of asking this question might be, "How
     does the Bible get the authority accorded it by devout Jews and
     Christians?"

   • An important extension of this question is, "What role should
     the Bible play, if any, in forming the views or sanctioning be-
     havior of the larger society? Should people who are not part of
     the faith traditions that consider the Bible sacred be expected to
     adhere to biblical norms of thought and behavior? This ques-
     tion underlies the questions in the current debates regarding
     the teaching of evolution or creationism in the public schools
     or the attempt a few years ago by an Alabama judge to place
     a monument containing the Ten Commandments in a govern-
     ment building.

3. Who has the right or responsibility to interpret the Bible?

   • Does every individual have the right and ability to interpret the
     Bible for himself or herself?

   • Does the church or religious community have that responsibility
     in some collective fashion?

3. LaHaye and Jenkins, *Left Behind*.

- Is Tradition* decisive for proper biblical interpretation and understanding?

- Is interpretation the preserve of the trained professional clergy and biblical scholars? Who decides?

4. How is that right or responsibility of interpretation properly exercised?

- What does the phrase "properly exercised" mean?

- Who has the authority to say what is the proper exercise? Any individual who reads the Bible? The faith community? The pastor or rabbi? Academic scholars who may or may not be believers?

- How is that interpretive authority managed or not managed? In other words, who judges whether a particular interpretation is valid or invalid, legitimate or not, and how is that judgment applied to the task of establishing ecclesiastical policies or defining norms of ethical behavior for people inside a particular faith community or even for people outside?

5. What are the consequences of this right or responsibility being exercised in ways that lead to radically different conclusions about what the Bible says or doesn't say?

For example, what are the consequences of certain Jewish and Christian groups' deeply held belief that the Bible entitles the Jews to possession of the land of Palestine, while others, both Jewish and Christian, deny that the Bible warrants such a claim? Or to take the example already cited, what would the consequences for public education and policy have been if the Kansas state legislature's earlier ruling that questions about evolution would no longer be asked on state exams had prevailed?

6. What does it mean to make the claim, "The Bible says. . ."?

This question has to do with the means by which a written text communicates meaning, particularly, in the case of the Bible, how it communicates meaning across distances of time, geography, and culture. Are there differences in the way the text of the Bible communicates meaning and the way another text (e.g., a play by Shakespeare or an op-ed piece from the *New York Times*) communicates meaning? It may be helpful here to break the question down into its constitutive parts.

- *How* does the Bible say something?

    This is a question that is often termed the hermeneutical question. Hermeneutics is the study of the history of the interpretation of texts and the principles of interpretation involved in the study of texts. Hermeneutical study attempts to understand *how* a text conveys meaning, and how the meanings conveyed have been perceived or understood by different cultures or in different periods of history. The number of hermeneutical studies of the Bible is phenomenal. The great third-century Alexandrian theologian and philosopher Origen was one of the first within the Christian community to address the hermeneutical question systematically. Robert Alter,[4] Sandra Schneider,[5] Walter Brueggeman,[6] and Francis Watson[7] are only a few of the scores of contemporary authors that have focused on the question of *how* the Bible says something.

- How does *the Bible* say something?

    This question focuses on the Bible as a particular text whose ability to convey meaning is seen to be of singular importance by many people. Observant Jews and Christians attach special importance to what the Bible, as opposed to what *People* magazine or the Baghavad Gita say. Even people outside these faith traditions who live in cultures heavily influenced by the history of biblical interpretation would agree that this is an important question. I've already mentioned that literary critic Northrop Frye, for example, though not writing as a member of the Christian faith community, nevertheless traces the influence, often deeply hidden, of the Bible on the shape of Western civilization. At a more popular level, Peter Gomes's *The Good Book: Reading the Bible With Mind and Heart*[8] explored the importance of the Bible in speaking to the concerns of people, including non-religious people in Western culture.

4. Alter, *The Art of Biblical Narrative*.
5. Schneider, *The Revelatory Text*.
6. Brueggeman, *Interpretation and Obedience*.
7. Watson, *Text, Church, and World*.
8. Gomes, *The Good Book*.

- How does the Bible *say* something?

    This way of putting the question is also part of the herme-
    neutical enterprise and is closely related to the question of *how*
    the Bible says something. However, by emphasizing the word
    "say" in the question, the focus is more on the way language
    conveys meaning and on the response of the hearer or reader of
    the text than on the literary mechanisms present within the text
    itself. The Bible will *say* something very different to a Christian
    or Jewish believer than it *says,* for example, to a secular scholar
    who is studying the Bible as a source of potential information
    about the cultic practices of ancient Semitic peoples.

7. What kind of claim is being made in the phrase, "The Bible says. . ."?

    - Is the person claiming to know what God wants?

    - Is that claim an implicit claim to be on God's side, or to have God
      on one's own side?

    - Is the claim being used legislatively? That is, is it attempting to
      impose the speaker's view on others around her? In other words,
      is it an authoritarian claim designed to trump the views or claims
      of one's real or imagined opponents?

    - Is the claim a more modest one— the community of faith or the
      individual is guided by what the Bible says, but not bound by it?

Many more questions could be raised; these will do for starters. Obviously, not all appeals to "The Bible says. . ." can be assessed in the same
way. The claim itself, as these questions reveal, is a formidably complicated one. In the following chapters, we will look at these questions in
more depth. I will not proceed through each of them systematically, but
in what follows, many, if not most, of them will be addressed.

Chapter 3

What Is The Bible?

Three Approaches to an Answer

What is the Bible? That may seem like a simple question. Yet a bit of thought will reveal that it is a much more complex and complicated question than it appears at first glance. The religious beliefs (or lack of them), the intellectual interest and formal training, or the socioeconomic location of the person answering the question may influence the answer. Some practicing Christians and Jews might immediately respond, "The Bible is the Word of God," though if pressed to unpack that statement would discover serious differences among themselves. Others might respond, "Well, the Bible is the record of our ancestors' encounters with God or beliefs about God. It's important for understanding our roots, but it has to be read critically and used with discretion today." People outside the Christian and Jewish faith communities might respond, "The Bible is an important collection of sacred literature that has had a profound impact in shaping Western culture." Still others might respond, "The Bible is a book sacred to Christians and Jews that is full of archaic, patriarchal, and often contradictory claims that have frequently led to violence, oppression of certain groups of people (particularly women and minorities), and religious intolerance through the centuries. It's time to bury it."

All of the above are possible answers to the question, "What is the Bible?" and all are answers that have, in fact, been promoted. Other answers, as well as other variations on these answers, are possible, depending on the individual to whom the question is put. Since I write as a Christian, I will confine myself in this chapter to discussing various

Christian answers to this question that have been put forward through the centuries. I do not limit myself to Christian answers out of a desire to exclude, but to avoid ignorantly misrepresenting the answers that persons outside my faith tradition might give. I believe, however, that within Judaism, and even within Islam, variations of the answers I will describe might also hold true.

For the purposes of simplification (some might say oversimplification), I am going to limit the discussion to three broadly-framed approaches to the question, "What is the Bible?" Within each one of these approaches, there are more specific and nuanced positions held by various individuals or groups. Nor are these approaches mutually exclusive. In fact, most Christians (and perhaps some Jews) would combine elements of all three broad approaches in their own understanding of the Bible, though one or another might be preferred. The three approaches begin from different starting points, and these differences in starting points influence not only the destination, but also the route in getting there.

The Confessional Approach: One Book, One Story, One Author

Probably the most common view of the Bible held by Christians, and the view commonly found in Bible study materials, Bible reading programs, and Sunday School curricula, this view treats the Bible as a single book, with a unified plot-line, the work of a single author, God, whose Word all the human writers express. There are many variations in the understandings of *how* God may be thought to be the author of the Bible and in the relationship between God and the human writers, but *that* the Bible is, in some sense, God's Word is probably believed implicitly by the majority of Christians. Even a cursory reading of the official statements on the scriptures in the formal doctrinal declarations of the various denominations found in the appendix at the end of this chapter will reveal how broadly such affirmations are shared even though the denominations or groups cited may be rather widely separated along the theological spectrum. There are many variations within this broad approach to understanding what the Bible is, ranging from the fundamentalist or literalist view of the Bible that believes every word of the text is "God-breathed" (inspired) and "factually" accurate, to those that read the Bible critically but still believe that its "message" (whatever that means) is divinely inspired. But all who give preference to the confessional approach would assert that God's definitive self-revelation and will is more-or-less contained within "The Holy Bible." The different understandings of *how* that is so are due to their different starting points.

For many, if not most, of those who view the Bible in this way, the Bible speaks with a single voice rather than a multitude of different voices. Knowledge of the historical setting of a particular biblical book, the cultural milieu, and the literary context may be useful for helping the reader correctly understand the supposed original meaning of the text. However, these will not significantly alter the view of those taking this approach, that from Genesis to Revelation, there is a coherent story line, described in some Christian circles as "God's Plan of Salvation." And God is the active agent in communicating this through the written text.

Five Implicit Assumptions

I call this the confessional approach because it begins with a confession of belief, *an affirmation about the Bible* which then controls how the Bible is read and understood. It does not arise out of a study of the Bible itself nor with a historical investigation of how the Bible came to be. It begins with a statement of belief: "I believe that the Bible is the Word of God." While such an affirmation of faith may be valid when properly understood, it is, sadly, mostly misunderstood and misused, and has given rise repeatedly over the centuries to various "Bible wars," contemporary versions of which are all too much with us today. For that reason, I will spend a little more time detailing five implicit assumptions in this first approach, in the hope that the dangers of using this approach as a starting point for understanding what the Bible is will be helpful.

1. The first assumption is that God is real. Obviously if there is no God, then to speak of any text as "God's Word," is absurd. A confession that the Bible is "God's Word," is implicitly a confession of faith that God is real. (I am trying to avoid using the term "exists" or "existence" with respect to God, since even those for whom God is a reality might not feel comfortable asserting that God "exists" like other beings exist.) Those beginning with the other two approaches to the Bible that we will examine may also share this assumption, though not necessarily.

2. A second assumption emerges from the first: that God is real, and has spoken or *revealed* the divine will and plan for human beings through these particular writings. It is one thing to argue, as the Deists of the eighteenth century (and some in the twenty-first century) did, the possibility of an impersonal "watchmaker" God who created the universe and set it in motion to run by inexorable natural laws and then went on eternal vacation, leaving the world to run itself without further divine interference or even interest. Such a God would have no cause to "speak" or to "reveal" anything to human beings other than what they are capable of discovering for themselves through observation of the operations of the various natural laws. To make one's starting point a confession that the Bible is "God's Word" is to confess belief in a God who stands outside or apart from the created order, and has intentionally communicated the divine will through a set of written texts. So the confession that the Bible is the Word of God is also implicitly a confession about the nature of the God whose Word it is believed to be. The phrases "divine revelation" or "special revelation" are often used by those who adopt this starting point. Again, this assumption may be shared by some who prefer one of the other two approaches to the Bible, but even those who do share it may vary considerably in their understanding of how such divine revelation works.

   While some who take the confessional approach would still acknowledge the humanity and fallibility of the human beings receiving the revelation, others would take a much more simplistic and authoritarian approach. "God said it; I believe it; that settles it," often seen on car bumper-stickers, is a slogan of extreme partisans of the confessional approach. The question of how an individual or community recognizes or discerns what it is that God is supposed to have said goes mostly unexamined or is deliberately ignored. The desire to put the Bible's authority beyond human questioning overpowers all other concerns. Interestingly enough, many who take this approach to the Bible often gravitate to churches where an authoritative (and even authoritarian) leader tells the faithful what God has revealed in the Bible.

3. A third hidden assumption in the confessional approach emerges: there is an inherent and essential significance to the order in which the biblical writings appear in our Bibles. Try to imagine how the

biblical "story" would read if the books of the Bible were in a different order. For example, what would happen to our perception of the plot line of the biblical story if Proverbs, Esther, Judges, Ruth, the books of the Kings and the Chronicles came at the end of the Old Testament, while the books of Isaiah and Jeremiah came where Judges, Ruth, Kings and Chronicles now appear? (This is, in fact, the way Judaism organizes its scriptures, though the actual books are the same as Protestants have in their Old Testament today.) Or, to take another example, suppose the Book of Revelation were the first book in the New Testament, and the Gospels were at the end. Would our understanding of the single story told by a single author (God) be the same or different if the arrangement of the writings in the Bible were different? The obvious answer is that our understanding might be different, and this brings to light the implicit assumption that the current arrangement is part of whatever makes the Bible "God's Word." In certain scholarly circles, the implicit assumption about the significance of the arrangement of the writings in the Scriptures is made explicit in references to "the canonical shape" of the text.[1]

4. A fourth implicit assumption is that the writings in our Bible *and no others* are *scripture,* i.e., sacred or authoritative texts for Christians and, for roughly two-thirds of the Bible, for Jews as well. Yet, the early Christian "Bible" contained some writings that are now accepted as scripture, by Roman Catholics but not by Protestants. These are books we commonly call the Apocrypha. What would happen to the assumption that the Bible has a unified and coherent plot-line or story-line if we were to add, for example, the books of Judith, Tobit, Wisdom of Ben Sira, Baruch, and I and II Maccabees to our Old Testament or some of the more recently discovered ancient Christian gospels such as the Gospel of Thomas or the Gospel of Mary Magdalene to our New Testament? For that matter, who decided how the present books in our Bible got there? We will examine that question in the next chapter.

---

1. Cf. Brevard Childs, *Introduction to the Old Testament as Scripture,* who appears to have introduced this term into the scholarly conversations about the Bible. Though he himself did not describe his approach as "canonical criticism," many subsequent followers did develop his thought and methodology in such a way that the new label stuck.

5. Finally (though there may actually be several more), one more implicit assumption comes into view: Some of those, particularly those who locate themselves on the right (fundamentalist) end of the spectrum of variations of the confessional approach, believe, not only that the Bible as we know it is holy scripture for Christians and Jews, but is holy scripture *for everyone else as well, whether they recognize it or not.* After all, if God has spoken, that divine word is for all humanity, and thus, those who accept the Bible as God's word have the responsibility of making that word known to others who either are ignorant of the Bible or reject it. In some Christian circles, this fuels a missionary thrust to persuade non-believers of the truth of the scriptural word through open proclamation, often termed "witnessing" or "evangelization." In others, it galvanizes efforts to translate the Bible into every known language in the conviction that anyone anywhere in any time or culture or circumstance will be drawn to the Christian faith if they only can read the Bible in their own language. In still others it fuels a desire to impose by whatever means, including the political process, their own understanding of that biblical message and have "God's Word" written into the laws of the land. It is not difficult to see the recent attempts of the judge in Alabama to erect a sculpture containing the Ten Commandments in the federal building in Alabama as an expression of this way of thinking about the Bible. Despite the hidden (or not-so-hidden) partisan political agenda in his actions, his belief that the "Law of God," as found in the Jewish-Christian scriptures, should be the law of the land is probably sincere.

Such theocratic and authoritarian approaches have a long (and frequently dishonorable) history. From the time of Constantine onwards, attempts to impose norms of thought and behavior derived from the Bible on society in general have led either to utopian programs that have failed dismally or to crusades and horrible forms of oppression under the guise of institutionalizing godliness. Examples are too numerous to count, from the church's creation of ghettoes for Jews in the Middle Ages to the massacre of the Cathars in southern France to Calvin's Geneva experiments to Cromwell's theocracy in England to the Puritans of Massachusetts in early America to contemporary attempts to reinstitute prayer in the public schools or post the Ten Commandments in public buildings and school classrooms. Inclinations toward theocracies are not unique to the Christian world, however. In fact, the separation of religion from political institutions is a modern (post-Enlightenment), and still somewhat rare, phenomenon. The current internal struggles within Islam over whether to impose the *shariah,* or religious law based on the Qur'an, on whole societies or nations, including upon non-Muslims living in those nations, as well as the tensions within Israeli politics between orthodox and secular Jews, are also examples of this implicit assumption about "God's Word." All of these struggles are biblical struggles.

As I said earlier, it is important to recognize that however attractive or meaningful the confessional answer to the question "What is the Bible?" may be, it is an answer that takes its departure from a belief that is asserted *about* the Bible *a priori* rather than being a conclusion drawn from the study of the Bible itself. There is no feature of the biblical writings themselves that demands such a view, as our simple experiment of rearranging the order of the books in the Bible demonstrates. The confessional answer begins with an affirmation or faith-statement that God is the real speaker in the Bible, and this affirmation controls how the Bible is viewed, read, and what the Bible is understood to say.

The Critical Aproach: Many Books, Many Stories, Many Authors

This approach to the question, "What is the Bible?" is very different from the confessional approach. This view does not start with a confession of belief in the Bible's divine origin. Rather, the real starting point for this position is the text of the biblical writings themselves and a "critical" or "empirical" approach to the investigation of those texts. *An important note: The word "critical" or "criticism" which appears in this section, including the description of the various scholarly methods of studying the biblical texts, does not imply a negative evaluation of the Bible.* Rather it is a term commonly used to refer to the well-developed methods of reading, analyzing, and drawing conclusions about texts. Many biblical scholars or academic scholars of religion hold something like this view of the Bible, as well as many pastors, rabbis, and members of the laity. Again, there is a great range of opinion among those who prefer this approach to the Bible. Some who are sincere adherents to their faith community, value the Bible as the sacred book of that community and therefore are committed in some manner to its "authority." Such empirical investigators of the Bible may accept that it conveys, in some real sense, "God's Word," though they might articulate that differently and would have arrived at that understanding in very different ways than do those who take the "One Book, One Story, One Author" approach. Others, who profess no religious belief at all, or even some of those who do, leave aside the question of whether or how the Bible may be "God's Word," but study the Bible in the same way and for the same reasons any other texts are studied. Some may bring to their investigations an implicit or explicit understanding of the Bible as primarily a human artifact that sheds light on particular events, peoples, and their religion, and which, therefore, deserves to be studied with the same critical tools one would apply to any other piece of ancient literature. Still others may begin with no confessional commitments one way or the other, but with a simple curiosity or desire for knowledge.

Whatever prior commitments those taking this approach might bring to their task, their starting point for the task itself is a careful and analytical study of the biblical texts, applying a variety of tools for textual analysis developed over the past few centuries. The critical approach begins with the observation of what is there, and then moves inductively to draw more generalized conclusions about the significance of what is there. To examine the Bible critically does not require, though it does not necessarily undermine, belief in the Bible's divine authorship, sacred status, or authority. The end or goal of such examination is varied, depending on the purposes of the investigator. One person may be interested in studying the biblical writings as examples of ancient literature, comparing them with other ancient documents contemporary with them or with modern examples of novels or histories. Another may be interested in known historical events contemporaneous with a particular biblical writing and on which that writing may shed light. Another may be interested in discovering how the biblical authors' own motives and agendas are revealed in their work. Yet others may actually wish to debunk the assumptions of much popular piety about the Bible or the faith of some Christians that springs from a particular use of the Bible. This is not to say that the critical approach is completely objective or neutral. Even the scientist most committed to empirical investigation does so within his or her own times and worldview and with certain presuppositions about the nature of reality, and those starting assumptions inevitably shape the scientist's understanding of her task and determines the shape and direction of the results of the quest. Where the knower stands determines, to a lesser or greater extent, what may be known, and this is true for scientists no less than for the rest of us. Objectivity may be a methodological goal of critical study, but it is only attainable in a relative sense. It is unfortunate that not all who approach the Bible empirically are aware of how their own subjective perceptions of reality and their own intellectual or spiritual presuppositions influence their conclusions.

Such blindness to the investigator's own presuppositions was graphically demonstrated at one of the sessions of the well-known "Jesus Seminar," perhaps the most widely reported contemporary scholarly effort to find "the historical Jesus" through careful historical research and critical reconstruction of the sources behind the gospels. It was the first session of the Seminar's work on the deeds of Jesus as recorded in the Gospels. In particular, the focus of that three-day meeting was on the stories of Jesus' exorcisms of evil spirits or demons. The major question on which the scholars were to vote at the end of the seminar was "Did Jesus perform exorcisms?" As the question was put to the Seminar, one of the scholars asked for clarification, "Are we supposed to vote on whether we think Jesus performed what he and the people of his day believed were exorcisms of demons, or on whether we think Jesus actually exorcized demons?"

The reply from the Seminar leaders was, "Interpret the question as you choose."

This response immediately "set the cat among the pigeons." One scholar objected, "But it makes a difference whether we think Jesus actually exorcized demons, or whether we can agree that Jesus and the people around him understood him to be exorcizing demons because that's the worldview they held."

Back came a reply from another participant: "Why does it matter?"

"Well, because ancient people believed there were actual supernatural beings called demons who could take possession of a person, and we don't believe that anymore."

From another voice: "Wait a minute, there are lots of people who still believe there are actual beings called demons."

Emphatic retort from first questioner: "Well, they're wrong!"

So much for "objective" empirical investigation! While much valuable knowledge has been contributed by the work of the Jesus Seminar to our understanding of the social, historical, cultural, economic, and psychological milieu of the world in which Jesus lived, the diversity of the portraits of "the historical Jesus" that have been produced by the Seminar's participants is testimony that even the most sincere efforts at objective historical investigation do not produce an assured result. Jesus has been variously portrayed as a Cynic sage, a Jewish peasant revolutionary, a prophet of Jewish Wisdom, a radical apocalyptic prophet, and a charismatic "spirit person," to name only a few of the more widely-publicized versions. While there is broad scholarly agreement on many of the details of Jesus' life, such as the fact that his characteristic form of teaching was parables, and a great deal has been learned about the nature of Jewish religion in Jesus' time, there is little consensus on Jesus' own self-understanding.

It is probably safe to say that those preferring the critical approach to the Bible would not believe that everything in the Bible is "literally" or "factually" true, in the sense that we might claim that the American invasion of Iraq in 2003 is a fact. They would accept that the Bible is a collection of diverse writings, written in diverse historical contexts, reflecting the beliefs, worldviews, and ideologies of their human writers. Like any other human documents, what the biblical documents say would be tested against other known facts about the world, and their content critically analyzed. Most practitioners of the critical approach would want to make a distinction between factuality and truth, recognizing that some literature might contain things that are not factually accurate but nevertheless convey truth. For example, the creation stories in Genesis would not be seen as factual accounts of how the world and the human race began, but as "stories of origin," told by the ancient Hebrews to explain to themselves who they were, who God was, and what their relationship to God meant, and why the world was the way it was. Their conclusions about God and the world might be deemed "true," in that they provided a reliable framework to live life meaningfully, but would not be deemed "factual" in the same way as the invasion of Iraq is factual. Or to put it another way, critical investigators of the creation stories of Genesis might accept that they contain important truths for life, even divinely inspired truths, while at the same time accepting the evolutionary explanation of the origins and development of life, including human life.

Critical or empirical study of the Bible makes use of a variety of investigative tools and approaches designed to aid the investigator in getting at the answers to the questions raised by the text under observation or which the investigator brings to the text. The following is a partial list of investigative tools and methods that have been developed over the past three centuries since the time of the Enlightenment, when the modern notion of historical reconstruction of past events first began to be developed. All of these and more are currently applied to the study of the Bible. Most biblical scholars use a combination of these critical tools rather than only one. The definitions below are greatly over-simplified, and those with expert knowledge in their use will find ample room to quibble. However, over-simplification notwithstanding, I offer them to the non-specialist reader for what they are worth.

Textual criticism is the study of the various manuscripts, manuscript families, and surviving fragments, of biblical texts, comparing one with another and with other ancient literature contemporary with the biblical text, with the aim of establishing the most probable form of the original biblical writing. Since no original autographs survive, all versions of the Bible in existence are composite texts built up by the patient and painstaking work of textual critics. Textual criticism is probably the least controversial of modern critical methods, and its results are widely accepted by those who, in other respects, differ greatly from one another in confessional stance or theological perspective.

Historical criticism makes use of the texts as sources for information about the historical events that lie behind them and to which they testify either directly or indirectly. Statements in the biblical text about events or places or people are also compared with statements in other texts roughly contemporary with the biblical writings. This involves making judgments about the degree of factual probability, depending on how the individual scholar (and often the collective judgments of the scholarly guild) evaluates the evidence and applies the criteria.[2]

Canonical criticism focuses on the present form of the Bible, reading individual texts within the Bible with awareness of the influence of the "canonical shape" of the whole. At the same time, canon critics pay attention to the history of the transmission and/or use of the text. How has this text come down through the centuries to us, and how has it been interpreted by past interpreters, particularly those within the community of faith that produced the canonical text?[3]

Form criticism is the study of short literary units or "forms" that frequently recur in texts (e.g., sayings, proverbs, miracle stories, etc.) as

---

2. Sometimes, "historical criticism" is erroneously presented as the only sort of biblical criticism other than textual criticism. Cf. John Barton's excellent and accessible book *The Nature of Biblical Criticism* for a much-needed corrective to this unfortunate tendency.

3. Joseph Ratzinger (Pope Benedict XVI) is particularly insistent on the value of "canonical exegesis" used in tandem with, but not limited by, historical criticism. Cf. *Jesus of Nazareth, Vol. 1*, xviii–xx.

windows into the experience, social settings, and agendas of the communities that produced the texts.

Redaction criticism: Redaction is almost a synonym for editing. This method focuses on the way biblical authors' intentions, motives, and agendas are revealed by the way they appear to have edited or modified whatever source material they were using. It presupposes that the human writers were not mere compilers of oral tradition, nor mechanical receptors of revelation, but actual authors who redacted or edited their source materials to advance their own points of view. In the study of the Gospels, redaction critics investigate the differences in the narratives of the same event by two different Gospel writers. The differences may be clues to the individual author's intentions. In the Gospel of Mark, for example, two motifs or themes occur that do not occur in the other gospels or occur much less frequently: the "messianic secret"—those passages where Jesus actively discourages those who recognize him as Messiah from telling others about him—and the portrayal of Jesus' disciples as consistently failing to understand him or recognize his true identity and mission.

Literary/Narrative criticism aims at an analysis of plot, characterization, juxtaposition, style, structure, irony, and genre in a text in order to discover new possible interpretations.

Rhetorical criticism examines the rhetorical devices an author uses to convey meaning such as the choice and arrangement of words, repetition of keywords or phrases, cultural symbols, patterns of argument, etc. Such analyses often reveal the author's ideological agenda or cultural mentality.

Audience criticism analyzes the writer's intended "audience" or attempts to identify the implicit and explicit audiences in the text to whom the writing is addressed. In the case of the Gospels, the particular audience to whom Jesus is portrayed as speaking (e.g., Pharisees, large crowd, disciples) provides interpretive clues to the author's historical context and agenda.

Reader-Response criticism studies, not so much the text itself, as the experience of a reader encountering the text, and through the act of reading/interpretation, becoming a participant in the creation of a "new" text where the primary focus is not on the intentions of the author—what the text meant—but the response it evokes or what it now does in the encounter with a particular reader(s).

Sociological/Anthropological criticism looks at the cultural and social milieus out of which particular texts emerged so that they may be understood in their social and historical context. One of the first such attempts at applying the disciplines of the social sciences to the study of the New Testament was Wayne Meeks's *The First Urban Christians,*[4] which analyzed the social, historical, and political context of the early Pauline communities.

Structuralist criticism, unlike all the methods listed above, is not so much a method of analyzing texts as a philosophical approach that is based on the revolutionary linguistic theories of Ferdinand Saussure and anthropologist Claude Levi-Strauss. Structuralists approach the study of anything from a conviction that reality is rooted in linguistics; human beings are "languaged" beings, and structure their world accordingly. The study of these ways of structuring reality sheds light on certain features of texts.

Postmodern criticism is a name for a variety of approaches to life in general, and to texts in particular, that begin from the point of view that there is no unshakeable foundation or starting point for making truth-claims. Every claim about truth is made from a *particular,* and therefore *contingent,* point of view. In simpler terms, we all start our investigation of something from where we are, and where we are inevitably determines to a lesser or greater extent what we will find. Postmodernism is skeptical of what it terms "metanarratives" or grand over-arching stories that claim to contain the whole truth. Since the world is full of such metanarratives, what empirical basis exists for choosing which of them is truer than another? It is also assumed that most people live within several overlapping metanarratives, some of which may be conflicting, thereby producing a greater or lesser degree of cognitive dissonance.

It will probably be clear by now that people who have a very strong preference for the confessional answer to the question "What is the Bible?" may find some of the assumptions and practices of those who prefer the critical approach threatening. If the Bible is "the Word of God," then who are we to analyze it critically and say whether or not it is true or factually accurate? How can something of which God is the Author be said to contain errors, even errors of fact? As I heard a seminary professor who held to the confessional approach once say, "If I admit that Luke may have been mistaken about Quirinius being governor of Syria at the time of Jesus' birth, how can I be sure he's not mistaken about the Virgin Birth?" Are those who begin with the confession, "God is the Author

4. Wayne Meeks, *The First Urban Christians.*

of the Bible," more faithful than those who begin with the assumption that the Bible is a collection of writings by people of faith which may be, and ought to be, studied analytically and critically? We should remember that each of these broad approaches to the question "What is the Bible?" includes a wide range of opinions that overlap and combine with one another. Not all who confess "The Bible is God's Word" do so with the understanding that every word in the Bible is factually accurate. (Postmodernists might be inclined to quibble with my characterization of something as "factually accurate," since the notion of "facts" is an invention of modernity.) Nor do all those who study the Bible critically and make negative judgments about the factuality of specific passages deny that God's Word is to be found in the Bible. We should resist the (perhaps natural) temptation to see these three approaches as polar extremes on a line.

God's Word _____Human words

A better way would be to think of them as interlocking circles, with areas that each holds in common with the others and areas in which each differs from the others. Each may share more in common with one than with another; the areas of overlap are not necessarily equal.

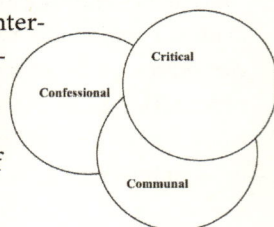

The Communal Approach: Communities Tell Their Stories

What I call the communal approach begins neither with a particular "confession of faith" about the Bible, nor with the empirical observation and critical analysis of the biblical texts themselves, but with the historical experiences of human communities—their conversations, arguments, and struggles to find meaning in their lives and circumstances, and the oral stories and written texts that are the product and record of those experiences. This approach recognizes that individuals and communities have the ability to reflect upon and interpret their existence and experience of the world, and in the process, come to regard certain writings that contain those interpretations as "scriptures." Since Christianity is one of the religions of the world, and most religions, at least the major ones, have writings that they consider sacred and authoritative, it may be useful to think about the historical processes and communally-shared convictions and traditions that are at work when a text or group of texts, in this case, the Bible, comes to be regarded *as scripture,* i.e., how texts, in general, function in communities, how certain texts become sacred, and how, in particular, the Bible functions as the scripture of Christian and Jewish communities.

This third approach begins with our historical experience of being human in the world. When we think about it, where else could we possibly start? Try as we may, we cannot go behind or before our experience of conscious existence in the world. I can say, "I believe that there is a realm of transcendent reality beyond my comprehension or experience of it and this reality has revealed itself to me as God." But it is I making that affirmation of belief. It is my brain formulating the thought and the sentence. We simply cannot get behind our own brains. Our consciousness, our historical being-in-time, is fundamentally where we must begin with anything.

Humans as Communal Beings

Consciousness, however, is never purely an individual phenomenon; it is socially constructed. From before birth, our knowing selves are linked first to our mothers and then to others who form the community into which we are born. The "I" who thinks my thoughts and speaks my words is a socially, as well as biologically, constructed "I." When the seventeenth-century poet John Donne said famously, "No man is an island," he was expressing this fundamental reality about our being. We are individuals by virtue of the fact that we are embodied, differentiated selves; our bodies do not occupy the same space as our mothers' or fathers' bodies, but neither are they wholly separate. Our parents' DNA is woven deeply into our own. To be human, then, is to have an individual consciousness of existence that is, at the same time, inescapably and fundamentally social. We are individuals-in-community from beginning to end, and cannot be otherwise. This existence as conscious individuals-in-community is *historical*—we exist in particular ways at particular times in particular communities that share particular geographical locations, cultural value systems, and beliefs. We have histories and we make history by our actions and choices.

Humans as Religious Beings

One aspect of our historical existence that appears to be universally shared is a sense that life is bigger or more mysterious than our ability to fully apprehend it. We sense this mystery at various times or in various circumstances or in diverse ways, but we become aware of this aspect of our conscious existence particularly when we encounter the boundaries of life such as birth, death, serious illness, dangerous accidents, sexual relationships, or other experiences that awaken in us an awareness of the mystery and fragility of our own existence. In each of these encounters with life's mystery, we may experience a sense of being confronted by something outside and beyond ourselves or more really real than ourselves, that becomes for us an ultimate point of reference, an organizing pole around which our very being is orientated. Such experiences are sometimes termed experiences of transcendence. Often we name this ultimate point of reference or ultimate mystery, God.[5] In other words, we are religious beings. We relate not only to ourselves, but to other people and the world around us, and we relate, through our encounters with the boundaries of our own existence, to that dimension of life that links us to "something beyond," or God.[6]

To help us grasp the significance of this approach to answering our question, "What is the Bible?" perhaps we can imagine a time before writing was invented. In the human story, writing is a very recent invention. Modern humans (*homo* sapiens) have existed for approximately 250,000 years, while writing, even in rudimentary symbol systems has existed for fewer than 10,000.

Prior to the evolution of writing, human communities existed in a world where sound and the human voice predominated. Communication

5. I am indebted to Gordon Kaufman (*In Face of Mystery*, 327) for this terminology and for his insights regarding human experience, though I do not necessarily endorse all of his conclusions or end in the same religious "place," that he does. Neither am I bracketing out the possibility of revelation; only that we cannot talk about revelation without beginning with our consciousness of something or someone that is revealed. We cannot start with that which is outside our own consciousness. Kaufman is surely correct in his notion that claims concerning revelation are often made primarily to trump the arguments of one's opponents.

6. At the time this manuscript was nearing completion, Robert Bellah's splendid book, *Religion in Human Evolution,* had just been released. I regret that I did not have it available earlier, since it is such a valuable resource. Readers familiar with the work of Habermas, Durkheim, Geertz, et. al., to which Bellah refers frequently, will recognize the family resemblance in much of what I cover in this chapter.

was primarily oral or gestural. Drawings or pictographs introduced some non-oral elements in communication, but the human voice was still the dominant means of communication. Each tribe or people had its own spoken language and culture. Each existed in very different circumstances due to differences in geography, climate, and relationships with neighboring communities. A desert-dwelling people from the Arabian peninsula would obviously experience and understand the world very differently than people who lived in the tropical rain forests of Borneo, for example. Not only their language and culture, but their very different life experiences, would shape their understanding of their "world." In fact, their language and culture themselves would be the products of their historical experiences of living in the desert or in the rain forest. The songs they sang, the stories they told, the sagas they rehearsed, would all be shaped by their "world."

To make this rather abstract notion more concrete, try to imagine how a people without a written language, located in the Arabian desert might describe themselves and their "world." Anyone who has ever been in the desert knows that the presence or lack of water is, quite literally, a matter of life or death. We might expect that the experience of thirst or a concern for having enough water to survive or the location of oases or wells would be common and frequent topics of discussion, as would the varieties of camels and their uses. The sense of openness, of trackless distances, of harsh and unforgiving nature is part of the experience, and hence, the language and culture of desert dwellers. In the religion of Islam, which emerged from the Arabian desert, paradise or heaven is often imagined as a particularly beautiful and lush oasis—a garden with abundant vegetation and numerous flowing fountains of water. (Interestingly, in the description of the New Jerusalem in the Book of Revelation, whose author was living on a small rocky island in the Aegean Sea, his vision of paradise includes this sentence, "And there was no more sea.") In the desert, the sky is immense and all-surrounding. It stretches out as far as one can see and the horizon touches it at every point of the compass.

Now imagine how people from the tropical rain forests of Borneo might describe the world around them. The sky would probably not figure as prominently in their vocabulary, since the jungle canopy effectively blocks a panoramic view of the sky. Vocabulary for trees and flowering plants and birds would be plentiful and diverse, although vocabulary describing different types of sand would not be nearly as common as they would be in the language of desert-dwellers. Discussions of the location

of oases would probably not ever occur, since water is an abundant com-
modity in the rain forest. And they probably could not even form a mental image of a camel. How might they respectively explain to themselves
and their children what the world was like, who they were, how they got
there, and their relationships to other peoples? Certainly we would expect their words and their sense of their own place in their world to be
described in quite different terms than those used by the desert-dwellers.

Let's extend our imaginative journey a little further. Suppose that
the desert-dweller had a child who wandered off and died of sunstroke
and dehydration. How might the bereaved parents explain or deal with
the experience of their child's death? Further, imagine a rain forest-dweller losing a child to a predatory crocodile in the murky swollen waters
of a jungle river. Despite the very great differences in the "worlds" that
the desert nomads and the jungle hunter-gatherers inhabit, and the corresponding differences in language and culture, they share the common
human experience of encountering one of life's boundaries—death—and
the bereavement that comes with it for the survivors. The historical
experience of losing a child, with its attendant grief, would call out for
description and explanation, an explanation that most likely would be
framed in religious terms. Humans are "meaning makers"; we can't help
ourselves. We look for patterns, for explanations, for reasons, as we relate
to the world in which we live and to the people who share it with us. How
many times have you said, or heard someone say, "I believe everything
happens for a reason?" This is a common modern expression in our culture that reveals our need to find meaning in our experiences.

Our descriptions and explanations of those meanings will be clothed
in the language of our culture and our communally-constructed picture
of our "world." The desert-dweller might say that an evil *jinn* (desert de-
mon) had stolen her child by luring the child away from the safety of the
tents into the waterless desert. The rain forest-dweller from Borneo might
think that an *antu* or evil spirit in the form of a crocodile had stolen his
child. Both would understand that the *jinn* or the *antu* belonged to the
realm of incomprehensible mystery, the same realm to which the fact of
death belongs. Their attempt to describe their experience of loss in reference to that mysterious realm of death is essentially a religious exercise.

Not all commonly shared human experiences would necessarily be
given the same religious significance in the two groups. Whittling an ar-
row to hunt game or making clay jars to hold water might be experiences
that our two very different peoples would share in common, but neither

group would necessarily attach the same degree of meaning to these mundane experiences as they would to the experience of losing a child. While it is possible that weaving rattan mats or making clay jars could be invested with religious or transcendent significance, it is unlikely that they would be so invested to the same degree as the confrontation with death and loss. Making mats or storing water may be necessary activities for making daily life easier, but neither brings the one who engages in those activities into confrontation with life's ultimate mysteries, even if they later become linked with those mysteries through religious rituals which make use of them as symbols (e.g., the bread and wine in Holy Communion or the shank bone and bitter herbs of the Seder meal). They are not "root" human experiences in the same way that childbirth or the death of a child are.

From these few examples, we can conclude that there are certain basic root experiences of human beings that are common to all cultures, world-situations or geographical settings in all times, and it is in these root experiences where religious language or references to God or the divine appears to be ubiquitous. Further back behind these root experiences it is impossible to go; we can only speak about them, in words, metaphors, or symbolic rituals. In fact, we might go so far as to conclude that it is impossible for human beings to think or articulate any thought or describe any experience without language, and the language used will be drawn from, and reflect upon, the "world" that provides the framework or "cultural landscape" for the experience being described. Or to put it another way, we can only tell stories, and our stories will be framed in the language of our unique, communally-constructed "world." Talk about God (or whatever terms are used to describe the confrontation with life's ultimate mystery) is talk that arises out of human experience and is expressed in human language. All language, therefore, is symbolic. It describes or explains something but is not the thing itself.

In the next chapter, we will look at how the writings in our Bible are the product of this historical process of meaning-making and story-telling, and how they came to be considered holy scripture.

Appendix: Official Denominational Statements on the Bible

The following statements on the scriptures are the official denominational positions derived either from those denominations' internet sites or from official church documents.

The Holy Bible was written by men divinely inspired and is the record of God's revelation of Himself to man. It is a perfect treasure of divine instruction. It has God for its author, salvation for its end, and truth, without any mixture of error, for its matter. It reveals the principles by which God judges us; and therefore is, and will remain to the end of the world, the true center of Christian union, and the supreme standard by which all human conduct, creeds, and religious opinions should be tried. The criterion by which the Bible is to be interpreted is Jesus Christ.

— **Southern Baptist Convention website**

Holy Scripture always has been for us the most authoritative guide to knowing and serving the triune God: Father, Son and Holy Spirit (Creator, Redeemer, Sustainer). As the divinely-inspired word of God, the Bible for us reveals our faith and its mandated practice.

— **American Baptist Convention website**

This church accepts the canonical Scriptures of the Old and New Testaments as the inspired Word of God and the authoritative source and norm of its proclamation, faith, and life.

—**Evangelical Lutheran Church in America website**

The Old and New Testaments, inerrant as originally given, were verbally inspired by God and are a complete revelation of His will for the salvation of men. They constitute the divine and only rule of Christian faith and practice. (2 Peter 1:20–21, 2 Timothy 3:15- 16)

— **Christian and Missionary Alliance website**

II. Under the name of holy Scripture, or the Word of God written, are now contained all the Books of the Old and New Testament, which are these:

(The list is omitted here for brevity; it is simply the list of our present books of the Bible, omitting the Apocrypha.)

All which are given by inspiration of God, to be the rule of faith and life.

—"Westminster Confession," Presbyterian Church in the USA

Of the Sufficiency of the Holy Scriptures for Salvation

Holy Scripture containeth all things necessary to salvation; so that whatsoever is not read therein, nor may be proved thereby, is not to be required of any man that it should be believed as an article of faith, or be thought requisite or necessary to salvation. In the name of the Holy Scripture we do understand those canonical books of the Old and New Testament of whose authority was never any doubt in the Church. The names of the canonical books are: *(list of our present biblical books).*

Of the Old Testament

The Old Testament is not contrary to the New; for both in the Old and New Testament everlasting life is offered to mankind by Christ, who is the only Mediator between God and man, being both God and Man. Wherefore they are not to be heard who feign that the old fathers did look only for transitory promises. Although the law given from God by Moses as touching ceremonies and rites doth not bind Christians, nor ought the civil precepts thereof of necessity be received in any commonwealth; yet notwithstanding, no Christian whatsoever is free from the obedience of the commandments which are called moral.

—"Articles of Religion," United Methodist Church, Church of England, Episcopal Church

From the saga of Adam and Eve to John's mystical vision of a new heaven and a new earth, the Bible tells the story of God's redeeming love. Holy Scripture provides the trustworthy and normative record of the history of salvation. Its luminous pages inspire, inform, and instruct the church's worship through all the centuries.

—United Church of Christ, *Book of Worship*

80. Sacred Tradition and Sacred SCRIPTURE, then, are bound closely together, and communicate one with the other. For both of them, flowing out from the same divine well-spring, come together in some fashion to form one thing, and move towards the same goal. [DV 9.] Each of them makes present and fruitful

in the Church the mystery of Christ, who promised to remain with his own "always, to the close of the age." [Mat 28:20 .]

81. Sacred SCRIPTURE is the speech of God as it is put down in writing under the breath of the Holy Spirit. [DV 9.] And (Holy) Tradition transmits in its entirety the Word of God which has been entrusted to the apostles by Christ the Lord and the Holy Spirit. It transmits it to the successors of the apostles so that, enlightened by the Spirit of truth, they may faithfully preserve, expound and spread it abroad by their preaching. [DV 9.]

—From the Roman Catholic Catechism

From Jewish traditions:[7]

Reform Jews accept the Torah as the foundation of Jewish life containing God's ongoing revelation to our people and the record of our people's ongoing relationship with God. We see the Torah as God inspired, a living document that enables us to confront the timeless and timely challenges of our everyday lives.

— Union of American Hebrew Congregations website

7. Of the four main branches of Judaism in the United States—Orthodox, Conservative, Reform, and Reconstructionist—only the Reform branch contains an official statement on scripture on its website. Judaism is more concerned with observance or practice than with doctrine. Especially in the Orthodox and Conservative traditions, the Mishnah (a compilation of historic rabbinic interpretations of the scriptures) is as important in establishing correct Jewish practice as the scriptures themselves. All accept Torah as the bedrock under Jewish practice, but the assumption is that Torah must be interpreted, and certain historic interpretations have scriptural authority.

Chapter 4

Three Stages Of The Word[1]

From Spoken Word to Written Text

In oral cultures, language is primarily *spoken* language. This may seem obvious, but since we are products of a literate culture, we may forget that the fundamental form that language takes for all of us is the production of certain movements of air through vibrating tissues in our throats that results in the intelligible sounds that we call speech. Even the seemingly pure mental activity of thinking depends on spoken words, and those spoken words (actual language as opposed to potential language) are given to us by the community into which we are born. Learning to speak is an imitative activity. Toddlers repeat virtually everything their parents or siblings say to them. Sometimes the context helps them understand the meaning; at other times, they simply repeat what they've heard with no real understanding of what it means. It's why grownups learn to be careful about what they say around very small children.

In predominantly oral cultures, rituals, dances, drama, and spoken words tell the stories in which the significant experiences of life are disseminated and remembered, particularly those given transcendent or sacred meaning or that help the community locate itself in its world. In

---

1. Anyone familiar with the work of Walter J. Ong will recognize immediately that this chapter title is also a chapter title in his ground-breaking work, *The Presence of the Word*. Although I am using the title in a somewhat different sense to describe the stages the word goes through on the way to becoming canonical scripture, I hope my use of it will acknowledge my own deep debt to Ong's seminal thought about language, literacy, orality, culture, and communication.

one sense, these oral tales or sagas or ritualized stories may be considered "texts," but they are texts that have but an instant of life. As soon as the sound waves produced in the telling dissipate, the "text" disappears. It may be held in the memory of a hearer, but invariably, when that hearer tries to reproduce it, it will not be verbatim, even when the speaker or hearer thinks it is. There have been numerous studies by ethnologists that confirm this phenomenon.

One of the most famous confirmations was the work of Harvard scholar Milman Parry and his graduate student Albert Lord. Before World War II, they studied and recorded long oral sagas sung by folk bards in isolated mountain valleys of the former Yugoslavia.[2] In their research, they recorded a saga sung by one bard, and then traveled several valleys over to another bard unknown to the first. They played the recording, and within twenty-four hours, the bard could reproduce the saga, often two to three hours in length, without missing any important information. However, when the recordings were compared, though the content was frequently the same, the songs were never repeated verbatim, *even though the bards thought they were.* This led Parry and Lord to conclude that memory operates differently in oral cultures, depending on themes, formulaic expressions, and keywords rather than word-for-word repetition of lines of written text. (An example of such formulaic memory hooks from Homer's *Iliad* would be his repeated expressions "the wine-dark sea" or "the golden-greaved Achilles.")

Writing changes things. Writing *fixes* language in silent marks on a surface, or in our electronic age, in an arrangement of pixels on an LCD screen. The word can exist without being turned into sound by the writer; silent marks on a page or a screen *stand for* certain sounded words. Writing appears to have developed as an aid to memory. When "the king was in his counting-house, counting out his money," he needed to remember where he was in the count, or he'd never know the value of his treasure, or which of his servants might have "sticky fingers." Many of the earliest examples of writing are essentially examples of such "counting"—inventories, lists of cargoes, etc. Writing is prefigured, perhaps, by drawing. The cave paintings of prehistoric humans, for example, pre-date hieroglyphics or cuneiform script, but are a step in that direction. We cannot know for certain what was in the minds of the people who painted the scenes of the hunt in the caves at Lascaux or Peche-Merle, but we can

---

2. Cf. Albert Lord, *The Singer of Tales.*

guess that at least part of the motivation may have been to preserve a record that could be communicated to others: to remember and tell a story in other words—literally in *other* words—*visible* words as opposed to *sounded* words.

As humans became more proficient in turning sounded speech into visible speech, writing became increasingly sophisticated, capable of expressing thought and experience with great subtlety, nuance, and abstraction. Writing became a tool for many other purposes, among them, connecting the stories of a people that help them to locate themselves in the world into larger narratives that over time would be edited, modified, or reinterpreted according to the needs of later generations, and, in many cases, appropriated by peoples outside the community of origin. Story-telling is fundamental to human beings, as Robert Bellah reminds us: "Human beings are narrative creatures. Narrativity, as we shall see, is fundamental to human identity."[3] Writing also enabled sharing more widely the "root" or "boundary" human experiences or, in the words of Paul Tillich, experiences that express our "ultimate concerns."[4]

From Written Text to Sacred Scripture

In our exploration of the communal answer to the question "What is the Bible?" we saw that the process by which certain writings eventually become sacred has cultural, religious, and historical dimensions. Scriptures are the products of communities of people who share a common *cultural* identity that provides the lens or filter through which they view themselves and their world and which shapes their understanding of reality. The *religious* dimension involves the need or desire to reflect upon human experiences of encounter with the mysterious nature of life and its meaning. Or to put it another way, religion is a search for an ultimate point of reference around which individuals and communities orient themselves to explain or make sense of life's experiences, particularly those universal experiences that deal with the limitations or boundaries of life—birth, death, transitions from childhood to adulthood, life-threatening dangers from accidents, natural disasters, serious illness, etc. Rites, practices, and beliefs then develop to express and maintain this religious dimension. The origin of these reflections on the sacred is *historical*, i.e., they arise

3. Robert Bellah, *Religion in Human Evolution*, 34

4. Paul Tillich, *Systematic Theology*, vol. 1, 323ff.

out of the concrete life of specific people in specific places, at specific times, and in specific circumstances. In many traditions, this encounter with the sacred "beyond" or "ultimate mystery" or "ultimate point of reference" is named God, though it is patently obvious that the word "God" or "god" does not mean the same thing to all those who use it.[5]

Judaism, Christianity, and Islam are monotheistic: this ultimate reality or ultimate point of reference is thought of as an indivisible unity. In these three traditions, this Holy One or Wholly Other is understood to be distinct from the world of finite creatures. Hinduism may ultimately be monotheistic as well, though its obvious polytheistic expressions often conceal this from those who are not adepts. In Hinduism, this indivisible unity's wholly-otherness or transcendence is minimized in favor of an emphasis on its immanence or fundamentally pervasive presence within all things, often termed pantheism. Buddhism does not directly address the question of the existence of God or gods, though at the popular level of practice, some forms of Buddhism assume a deity or deities.

In Judaism, Christianity, and Islam, God is frequently referred to in personal and political terms such as Creator, King, Lawgiver, Master of the Universe, Holy One, Father, Redeemer or Savior, or, less frequently, in more abstract philosophical terms such as Ground of Being, First Cause, or Being Itself. In the Book of Exodus, as Moses stands before the burning bush, in his encounter with this Wholly Other, he asks, "Whom shall I say sent me?" And the Wholly Other replies, "I AM" (or perhaps more accurately "I will be whom I will be"). This name in Hebrew consists of four consonants (tetragrammaton), transliterated as YHWH, and it quickly became in Jewish practice a name too sacred to speak aloud. When this name first appeared in older English translations such as the King James Bible, it was rendered Jehovah, which is a combination of the four consonants of the name combined with the vowels of the word *adonai* (Lord), which Jewish scribes often wrote in the margins to alert a reader to vocalize *adonai* rather than speak the unspeakable Name. In contemporary English translations, it is usually simply rendered as Yahweh or LORD God (note the use of small caps font). Specifically, YHWH is the name for the God of Israel, and is not to be confused with the gods

5. Cf. Robert W. Jenson, "The Father, He . . .," where Jenson argues that the meaning of the word "God" is narratively established, and thus cannot mean the same thing universally. In Jenson's view, the attempt to universalize the meaning of "God" by according the term metaphorical weight rather than the specificity of a proper name grounded in a communal narrative is a characteristic of gnosticism.

of ancient Israel's neighbors. Claims about the ultimacy or exclusivity of a particular religious tradition's name for God is a different question, and one that is far beyond the scope of this essay.

In other religious traditions, e.g., the various forms of Buddhism and some other Eastern cultures, this ultimate mystery of life or ultimate point of reference is not conceived in such personal terms, but rather as Emptiness or The Void. This naming of the ultimate mystery or that-which-is-beyond is bound up with culture and language, i.e., it cannot be named apart from the language and culture in which this encounter takes place.[6]

This explains why, in the Jewish scriptures, God is frequently conceived as a Warrior who fights on behalf of his people and defeats Israel's enemies. "Yahweh Sabaoth," means literally, "LORD God of Hosts [or Armies]." Why would the Israelites name God in this manner? Because Israel, at the time, was engaged in rather constant warfare with neighboring peoples, particularly the Canaanites, and was in the process itself of becoming a settled people ruled by a warrior-king instead of a wandering group of nomadic goatherds. Had Israelite culture and religion not developed in the context of warring groups of people ruled by militaristic kings, it is unlikely that the name LORD God of Armies would have suggested itself to them as the name for that which they considered the ultimate point of reference for their communal life and identity as a people. The historical experiences of Israel's life provided the reservoir of concepts and symbols from which they drew to reflect upon the meaning of those experiences.

The historical reality involves more than simply providing the reservoir of symbols and concepts; it also refers to the process by which certain reflections on these religious experiences come to be normative and sacred. As people reflect on their experiences and give voice to them in song, story, saga, art, and eventually (following the invention of writing) in literary texts, there is a sifting process by which some texts are accorded special significance because they are recognized as containing particularly profound or desirable reflections on the experiences of the

6. This is how I conceive the value in Jenson's insistence that "God" is not a universal metaphor, but possesses a specific identity narratively established. It also precisely establishes the differences between Judaism's, Christianity's, and Islam's conceptions of God. While the three share a common narrative, they do so only to a certain point. Beyond that point, their narrative differences, arising out of differing historical circumstances and cultures, are decisive for their particular understandings of God and the moral, ethical, and cultural values and actions rooted in those understandings of God.

community, both past and present. These writings are specific to a particular people, a particular culture, a particular language (though later translations may occur), and like the people who produce them, texts have a history, i.e., the way they are perceived, used, interpreted, and transmitted changes through time.

The so-called "servant songs" in chapters 42–53 of the Book of Isaiah are an example of this historical process of perception, use, and transmission at work. Scholars have long identified four passages (42:1–4; 49:1–6; 50:4–9; 52:13—53:12) as forming a distinct group of oracles within the larger work. These distinctions are not always apparent in English translations, but in the Hebrew text are easily distinguished by differences in form, structure, meter, and content from their surroundings. At some point, they were interwoven with the other material in this section of Isaiah, and may or may not have been written by the same author. We may safely assume that the author of these passages knew what he meant when he spoke of the "servant of the Lord" who was "wounded for our transgressions, bruised for our iniquities . . ." We cannot be as certain that *we know* what he had in his mind as he wrote those texts, as subsequent attempts to identify the "servant" have shown. The prophet himself, Israel (often poetically personalized as "Jacob"), or a faithful minority within Israel have all been proposed as the identity of the "servant of the Lord," and all are plausible interpretations that Jewish and Christian interpreters have advanced. Many early, as well as later, Christian interpreters have proposed a fourth possibility for the servant's identity: that the prophet really was referring (either consciously or unconsciously) to the future Messiah Jesus, a reading that most Jewish, as well as some Christian, interpreters, particularly those committed to a historical-critical reading of the texts, have strenuously resisted. What we do know is the way the servant songs have functioned or been used within both Judaism and Christianity. We can see how commentators and preachers have treated them, as well as the way they have been treated by painters, musicians, and others. In other words, we can trace the history of the text—its uses and interpretations.[7] Indeed, one could almost make the case that more popular Christology has been learned from singing or listening to Handel's *Messiah*, which makes extensive use of the "servant songs," than from either the scriptures or theologians.

7. Cf. John Sawyer's fine work on Isaiah, *The Fifth Gospel*, 1996, for an original and fascinating study of the influence of Isaiah, particularly II Isaiah, on Christian theology, art, religious practice, and liturgy.

Within the history of Jewish use of those texts, the most common understanding was that the "servant of the Lord" was Israel itself. Steeped in the stories of God's covenant with Abraham, the Exodus, and the giving of the Law, many Jews understood the mission of Israel to be a "light to the Gentiles," becoming a faithful model of how God intended human beings to live, so that all nations would come to know and worship the God of Israel as the true and living God. These writings were important for Jews who read and meditated on them because they illuminated what it meant to be faithful to God, and what such faithfulness might require. Over time, because of this ability to illuminate and inspire beyond their immediate setting and context, these texts acquired a sacred, normative quality; they became "scriptures."

The earliest Christians (who were Jews) *already* accepted Isaiah's writings as "holy scripture." By the time the Gospels were written in the latter third of the first century of the Common Era, these "servant songs" had become a source for Christian meditation and reflection on the meaning of the death of Jesus, so much so that they shaped the very way the Gospel writers told the story of Jesus' sufferings. There is no indication within any Jewish writing prior to the emergence of the Christian movement that this "servant of the Lord" image was ever identified with a heavenly messianic individual. Even in the earliest Christian writings, those of St. Paul (mid-first century CE), there is no indication that Paul read these "servant songs" in Isaiah as being predictive foreshadowings of Jesus and his sufferings. But by the time of the writing of the Gospels (ca. 70–90 CE), this interpretive move had become solidly established. And from that point onward, for Christians, those songs have always been profoundly meaningful, and frequently viewed as though they were actual predictions of Jesus's death that Isaiah was making under divine inspiration, even though admittedly without the author's awareness that he was talking about Jesus. In fact, it is virtually impossible for Christians now to read these "servant songs" without thinking of Jesus. This way of reading these texts is deeply embedded in the Christian history of biblical interpretation.

A true story will illustrate just how deeply. A colleague was taking a course on the Old Testament prophets at a prestigious theological seminary in the eastern United States. The professor, who was a well-known Christian Old Testament scholar, was "delivering his soul" on one of his pet peeves—the common (and in his view, indefensible) Christian interpretation of Isaiah 53, the Song of the Suffering Servant, as a reference to

Jesus. After thoroughly disabusing his students of any such anachronistic and parochial views of that prophetic oracle, he was about to move on, when my colleague raised his hand and asked, "Prof, what passage of scripture do you read in church on Good Friday?" The professor, with a somewhat furtive grin, replied, "Isaiah 53, of course."

To the Jews, however, to this day, no such meanings are found in these songs. To Jews, they are "scripture" because they illuminate the meaning of Israel's calling and mission; to Christians, they are "scripture," because they illuminate the meaning of Jesus's sufferings as a key to understanding God's redemptive plan. In both cases, a historical process of reading, interpretation, and transmission has been at work over a relatively long period of time.

The consideration of a text as "scripture" is something that accrues to certain writings as part of such a historical process; it is not something that is self-evident within the writings themselves or a "given" at the time of their production. No author of a writing that is currently contained in our Bible was aware that he or she was writing sacred scripture. Even if a particular author felt "inspired" to write what he considered a message from God, there was no way he could have known that later generations would treat his message as "scripture," thus recognizing its inspired character. When a particular writing eventually does attain the status of "scripture," there is often an assertion that it was divinely revealed or inspired, suggesting that its origins are from beyond the human historical plane, but this is simply a way of recognizing or reinforcing the sacred status it has achieved over the course of time.

Wilfred Cantwell Smith's views on this process are illuminating. After making the point that just as not every plant is termed a weed, but only plants that grow in an unwanted location without being cultivated, and just as no woman can be a wife in and of herself, but only in relation to another person who is her spouse, so

> . . .no text is a scripture in itself and as such. People— a given community— make a text into scripture, or keep it scripture: by treating it in a certain way. *I suggest: scripture is a human activity* [Smith's italics]. . . . The quality of being scripture is not an attribute of texts. It is a characteristic of the attitude of persons—groups of persons—to what outsiders perceive as texts. It denotes a relation between people and a text. Yet that too is

finally inadequate . . . At issue is the relation between a people
and the universe, in the light of their perception of a given text.[8]

To sum up, this historical process of scripture-making begins with an
author writing a text with a particular audience in mind. This audience,
and subsequent audiences within the same cultural/linguistic world read
meanings into and out of this text, and if those meanings are deemed
sufficiently profound or significant in the way they illuminate human life
and human encounters of the members of the community with life's "ultimate concerns" or religious experiences, they become, over time, holy
scripture.

Once the text is treated as scripture, then it takes on a life of its own
and has weight or authority—it becomes a norming norm—both for the
audience from which it emerged and also for future audiences, some of
whom may be far removed from the original cultural/linguistic world out
of which the text came. The status of the text *as scripture* then determines
the quality of attention paid to it and influences the meanings that are
read into and out of it by later audiences, even audiences to whom earlier
meanings are unknown or lost in the mists of time past. Few contemporary Christians, apart from professional scholars, are aware of how
Philo or Irenaeus or Augustine interpreted a given scriptural text, though
their own community leaders or pastors may very well have absorbed
those interpretations from their own teachers. Texts become scriptures
because of the way they illuminate human experience, and they continue
to illuminate human experience across time and culture because they
are recognized as scripture. Eventually, this leads to some more formal
delineation of the text as scripture, i.e., there is some official recognition
or approved list (canon) drawn up of those texts that meet the criteria
above, and it is to this next stage of the word that we now turn.

From Scripture to Canon[9]

The process by which two religious communities, Judaism and Christianity, decided which of their writings that were already *deemed* to be

---

8. Smith, *What Is Scripture?*, 18.

9. The research into the emergence of both the Jewish and Christian canons is vast.
My own attempt to lead us through a process of thinking about how the scriptures of
Judaism and Christianity developed into their present form, depends heavily on that
research. Very little in this chapter is original with me, but is simply what is, and has

scripture really and finally deserved that honor, and were therefore accorded unique authority, was long and complex. This process is often termed "canonization," and the list of scriptures accepted as uniquely authoritative by a particular community is termed the "canon." Canon means measure or standard; canonical scriptures are those, therefore, that "measure up" to a particular standard in the view of the community that adopts them. Canonical scriptures are also, at a later stage in the process, those writings against which the community's teachings, rituals, and practices are measured.[10]

The earliest Christians were Jews and, therefore, already possessed a collection of sacred writings that they deemed to be holy scripture. These were the writings that Christians now commonly refer to as the Old Testament or that Jews refer to as *Tanak* or, simply, the Bible. The earliest Christians, however, did not initially refer to these writings as the Old Testament. If they called these writings *collectively* any name at all, it was simply *tēs graphēs,* (singular: *hē graphē*) which is the Greek term meaning "the scriptures" or simply "the writings." There were Jewish writings that gradually had gained scriptural status by th fifth century BCE, but no official Jewish list of scriptures existed until well into the Christian era. Likewise, there were Christian writings that later became scriptures from the mid-first century onwards, but no officially defined Christian canon until the late fourth century CE, at the earliest. The first use of the term "canon" to refer to a widely approved list of scriptures, doesn't occur until 397 CE, in Bishop Athanasius of Alexandria's *Festal Letter 39.* The terms "scriptures" and "canon" are related, but not identical. Though in popular

---

been, widely known and accepted by biblical scholars for some time. I have relied primarily on the work of Freedman and Sundberg in their articles on the canon in the *Interpreter's Dictionary of the Bible, Supplementary Volume,* the articles of Sanders and Gamble in *The Anchor Bible Dictionary,* Metzger's magisterial *The Canon of the New Testament,* and Barton's *Holy Writings, Sacred Text.* These sources contain most of what is now common knowledge about the canon as well as individual insights into that process.

10. A recent blog in the *New York Times* by Professor Stanley Fish about "legal canons" as guiding interpretive principles for correctly reading legal documents appears to have some overlap with the function of the biblical canon. (See Fish, "Intentions and the Canon.") While Fish is using "canon" more in terms of specific interpretive principles rather than as an authoritative collection of writings, this notion applies to the biblical canon as well. Because the canon is the church's authoritative list of scriptures, not unlike the U.S. Constitution, the church has evolved certain canons of interpretation that (largely unconsciously) govern the way a person reads the Bible if one is a practicing member of the faith community that holds the Bible sacred.

usage we sometimes use these terms interchangeably, for the purposes of thinking through the process of canonization, it will be helpful to keep them separate in our minds. "Scripture(s)," are those individual writings or collection of writings that have gained the status of holy or sacred because of the broad agreement on their importance and widespread use within a particular religious community. "Canon" refers to a collection of scriptures that has been delimited by the community—these particular scriptures and no others. Professor Bruce Metzger has given us a useful way to keep these terms straight: "Scriptures" is a collection of authoritative writings. "Canon" is an authoritative collection of writings.[11]

Today, when we speak of "the Bible," we refer to the form this authoritative collection takes as a single volume bound between two covers. Earlier, we focused on the first part of Metzger's definition—how certain writings came to be regarded as authoritative writings or scriptures. Here we are focused more on the second part of the definition— how certain scriptures came to be placed in a bounded, exclusive, and authoritative collection or canon.

Although a formal fixing of the list of Jewish scriptures had not yet occurred by the time of Jesus and the apostles, there was a *de facto* canon in use and evolving. A couple of centuries before the time of Jesus, Jewish scholars in Alexandria had translated the Hebrew scriptures into common Greek. It became known as the Septuagint, often abbreviated as LXX, because Jewish tradition held that there were seventy translators, corresponding to the seventy known nations of the world. By the time the Jesus movement began the Septuagint was in wide use, even in Palestine, since few people except scholars could read Hebrew any longer (Hebrew was no longer a living spoken language). The Septuagint differed from the Hebrew manuscripts in that it included some late Jewish writings known as the Apocrypha, originally written in Greek rather than in Hebrew and considered heretical by some Jews, though held in high esteem by others. Philo, a Jewish contemporary of Jesus who was a renowned scholar in Alexandria, even thought the translators were divinely inspired. Other Jews, however, particularly those in the rabbinic tradition, eventually opted to stick with the Hebrew texts of their scriptures. The Septuagint was the "Bible" of early Christianity, and is essentially identical to what Christians have historically called the Old Testament. The early Christian

11. Bruce Metzger, *The Canon of the New Testament*, 1, though Metzger acknowledges that canonical scholars sometimes are divided over which of the two statements actually describes what is meant by the canon.

writers, including all those whose writings now comprise the New Testament, always quoted from the Greek version, and usually with the phrase reserved for citing texts regarded as authoritative scripture, *gégraptai*, "it is written." John Barton has argued that if we study the citations of Jewish texts within the New Testament and the early church Fathers, we will discover that one of the main, if not *the* main, criteria for regarding a text as scripture was simply how old it was.[12] If it was old enough, it was "scripture," and cited as such—"it is written" or "as was spoken." A text that survived over time was one in which succeeding generations found meaning and answers to their own fundamental questions. This ability of some texts to be perceived as significant beyond their own time and circumstances, particularly as they enable the community to understand itself in relation to God, is a major criteria, as we have seen, in it being considered "holy scripture."

It is important not to make a mistake that has often been made in trying to reconstruct the history of the emergence of the biblical canon, i.e., assuming that the early Christians who were citing the Jewish scriptures and the writings of other early Christian writers, had in mind some notion that they were developing a fixed list of scriptures. That is an anachronism. The growth of the canon was just that—growth. It was an organic process, in which certain writings were used more frequently than others and certain ones fell into obscurity. Some were accepted because they purported to be written by someone famous or revered, particularly an apostle or known associate of an apostle. Others were rejected because their authors were unknown or despised; the content of some was widely recognized and agreed to, while the content of others reflected the thinking of a minority. Attitudes toward particular writings underwent shifts—at one point, looked upon more favorably and at another, less favorably. These fluid attitudes gradually hardened in the direction of either common acceptance or rejection. In some cases, deliberate decisions were made about including or excluding certain writings within authoritative lists, though these came late in the process rather than earlier, and only after there had grown up a consensus about a body of texts

12. John Barton, *Holy Writings, Sacred Text*, 64–68. Barton makes the interesting and important observation, based on the frequency of citations, that while the Jewish scriptures were recognized by the early church as holy scripture, they were not as important for early Christian thinking and life as the Gospels or the writings of Paul, even though these Christian writings were much more recent and had not yet attained the status of scripture. The Christian writings were cited many times more frequently in the arguments of the Apostolic Fathers and the Apologists.

that were generally agreed upon or deemed to be scripture. The Bible, as we know it, is something that we modern Christians take for granted, as though there must have been some grand design on the part of the earliest Christian community to produce such an authoritative collection of writings. We can only see the shape of the canon clearly in hindsight. At the time, there was simply the use, or lack of use, of certain writings that were accepted as scripture or not, and this situation remained fluid to a certain extent at least through the end of the fourth century. Criteria for how an *authoritative writing* became part of an *authoritative collection* of writings evolved gradually over time in an organic fashion.

Emerging Criteria for Canonicity

When we speak of the criteria used to determine whether a writing was canonical or not, we should not imagine a small committee sitting around a table, operating from a checklist previously drawn up. These criteria were very informal, fluid, and emerged from particular historical circumstances or in a variety of settings, including worship, catechism, evangelism, and apologetic writing. Sometimes, an ancient writer would state explicitly why he accepted or rejected a particular writing, and frequently more than one of the developing criteria operated simultaneously. It is by looking back that historians can make educated judgments about the various factors that were influential in determining what stayed in the canon and what did not.

1. Apostolic authority was a strong criteria. This did not necessarily mean authorship by an apostle, but rather that the authority of an apostle stood behind a writing, or that the church recognized the writing as containing genuine apostolic teaching, based on the memories of those who knew one or more of the apostles.

2. Catholicity was another criteria: was the writing applicable to the church as a whole and not just to a particular group, sect, or local situation?

3. Agreement with what the church recognized as correct teaching was an important issue. In other words, in the early church, scripture was not the measure of correct teaching; correct teaching was the measure of whether a writing was scriptural. It was the *regula fidei* or rule of faith that consisted of the teachings transmitted through preaching, worship, catechism, and liturgy that was the standard

against which particular writings were measured and judged to be canonical scripture or not. (Notice that a writing could be considered scripture but not be canonical.) As time went on, however, this relationship between scripture and church teaching became more reciprocal. If "correct teaching" or "the rule of faith" was a measure against which texts were judged to be scriptural or not, once those texts were widely accepted, they in turn became a measure (canon) against which the church's teaching had to be tested.

4. Customary usage was yet a fourth criteria: had a writing been in widespread use from early times? If a writing had stood the test of time in providing meaningful reflection on the experiences of succeeding generations of the religious community, it stood a good chance of being included.

One characteristic that was *not* a criteria for inclusion in the canon was inspiration. Since inspiration was given to persons and to the church as a whole, it did not attach exclusively to writings, nor was inspiration a characteristic exclusively of canonical writings. Authors could be inspired to write, but inspiration did not necessarily get them into the canon (e.g., the *Didachē*; also St. Matthew in 2:23 cites *as scripture* a statement from a writing that is completely unknown and which is not found in either the Jewish or Christian canon). The modern fascination with inspiration stems from two principal sources: the first is a misreading, or at least an overdependence on, 2 Timothy 3:16. While it can be rendered as "All scripture is inspired by God and is useful . . .," it can also be just as legitimately rendered as "All God-inspired scripture is useful . . ." Even if the first rendering is accepted, we have already seen that inspiration attached primarily to the author or the interpreting community rather than to the writing itself. The second source was the rationalistic view of the Bible that was adopted by early twentieth-century fundamentalism, in which the texts themselves were understood to be "verbally inspired," or inspired in some "plenary" fashion in an attempt to put them beyond the reach of the newly-developed (and threatening!) scholarly discipline of historical criticism. This insistence on the inspiration of the texts is a thoroughly modern concern; it was not a concern of the earliest Christians when they were making decisions about what to include in the canon.

For quite some time, biblical scholars have recognized a paradox in the history of the Christian canon: despite possessing a collection of sacred scriptures which they and their fellow Jews recognized as authoritative, even God-inspired, the early Christians, particularly those in the latter third of the first century and well into the second century, made much less frequent use of those common scriptures than they did the writings that other Christians had produced or were producing (e.g., Paul's letters, the Gospels, etc.), *despite the fact that these Christian writings were not yet considered by them to be holy scripture*. Moreover, the writings which they always cited as "scripture" (*hē graphē*) were those of the Septuagint (Greek version of the Jewish scriptures), which did not follow the three-fold order of Torah, Prophets, and Writings that the Hebrew version did, but were arranged in the order that Christian Old Testaments are today.

If we were to try to think of a comparable situation today, it would be as though contemporary Christians engaged in current theological and ethical discussions cited the writings of Marcus Borg or Brian McClaren or Rick Warren more frequently than the Bible. (This may well be the case, in fact.) The fact that the second-century Apologists and Apostolic Fathers cited the writings of Paul and the Gospel writers more than they cited the writings they already regarded as holy scripture indicates that for those Christians, the stories and events surrounding the life and death of Jesus were more foundational to their thinking, believing, and practice than the scriptures they had inherited from Israel.[13]

In particular, the sayings of Jesus were highly valued, and the gospels, both the canonical gospels and the other early Christian gospels, were primarily written to preserve the stories of Jesus's acts, and particularly, his sayings that had been passed down orally, even though both oral storytellers and writers felt free to expand, alter, or otherwise edit those stories and sayings to suit their own narrative purposes. Oral tradition, particularly as it has developed in the West (though not so much in rabbinic circles) is by nature remarkably fluid and flexible, much less concerned with verbatim transmission than with meaning that can be flexibly applied to a variety of situations or authorial concerns.[14] It is probably not an exaggeration to say that the principal reasons the early Christians continued to read the scriptures of Israel at all were 1) it was these scriptures that provided them the vocabulary, concepts, and narrative "world" (the stories of God's dealings with Israel) that enabled them

13. Cf. Ibid., 67–68.

14. Cf. Ibid., 102–104, where Barton argues for different kinds of approaches to oral materials, some of which are treated loosely and paraphrased or altered freely, and some, as in much of the rabbinic tradition, treated extremely tightly, insisting on precision and accuracy.

to speak about their understanding of Jesus, and 2) because they were able, successfully, to reread and reinterpret those scriptures in light of their experience of Jesus, i.e., they "Christianized" the Jewish scriptures. *The Jewish scriptures (Old Testament) for Christians, and particularly for Gentile Christians after the first generation, gained their legitimacy from the church's beliefs about Jesus rather than the other way round.*

In a sense, this is a kind of backhanded witness to the early Christian experience of what they came to call "the resurrection of Jesus from the dead." The experience of St. Paul that he understood as a visionary encounter (cf. Gal 1:11–17) with a (now) living Jesus after the crucifixion, as well as the reported experiences of others who claimed that Jesus had *appeared* to them, was the initiating or motivating impulse that led Jesus's own disciples, Paul, and the next generation of followers (the generation of the Gospels) to go back to their scriptures to find ways to make sense of their experience.[15] The language of resurrection was already present within Judaism, particularly within the Pharisaic tradition, so it was hardly surprising that Paul and others found it convenient to describe what they believed happened to Jesus by that term. If the scriptures of Judaism provided them with the language and concepts by which to name that experience and reflect on it, it was those in-house reflections themselves, whether oral or written, that became most important to them, even though these in-house reflections were not yet considered "scripture."

The terms "Old Testament"[16] and "New Testament," which began to be used late in the second century, did not originally refer to the canonical written texts. Rather, the terms, as used by Melito of Sardis and Clement of Rome, referred to the belief that God had entered into covenant, first with Israel, and later with the church. When applied to the Jewish and Christian scriptures, the meaning was that these writings belonged either to the old or the new covenants, not that the writings themselves were covenants. As time went on, however, and the Christian writings gradually attained the status of holy scripture by being cited as such, it was natural that the terms Old Testament and New Testament would

---

15. Cf. Kenneth Cragg, *What Decided Christianity*, for a somewhat dated but still valid argument for the primacy of early Christian experience in the articulation and development of theology and Christology. Cf. also Luke Timothy Johnson, *Religious Experience in Earliest Christianity*, for a similar emphasis.

16. The word testament is the Latin translation (*testamentum*) of the Greek word *diathēkē*, which means covenant.

begin to refer to the writings themselves rather than to the covenants with God they were understood to represent.

The shape of the canon is still not "set in concrete." Throughout the history of the church, there have been disputes about certain of the canonical writings. Martin Luther thought the Epistle of James and the Book of Revelation should be excluded from the canon—James because, in his view, it was a writing of Jewish legalism that taught (against Paul and Peter) salvation by works. He objected to Revelation because "Christ is neither taught nor known in it. But to teach Christ, this is the thing which an apostle is bound above all else to do; as Christ says in Acts 1, 'You shall be my witnesses.' Therefore I stick to the books which present Christ to me clearly and purely."[17] This may tell us more about Luther's ignorance of the literary conventions of apocalyptic literature than it does about the Book of Revelation.

In our own day too, the canon is again the subject of discussion. Some feminist theologians who maintain that the only writings retained in the canon were those chosen by men in strongly patriarchal societies, are arguing for the inclusion of other early Christian writings, particularly those that emerged from so-called "gnostic" circles, that appear to give a higher status to women. Elaine Pagels, a scholar at Princeton University, published her well-regarded *The Gnostic Gospels*, and more recently, *Beyond Belief*, to argue the case that early Christianity was much more diverse and produced many more sacred texts than most Christians are aware of, many of which are more friendly to women than the canonical writings. Bart Ehrman, in *Lost Christianities*,[18] makes a similar case for the wide spectrum of belief and practice in the early church. The more recent discovery of the second-century *Gospel of Judas* has also reinforced the understanding of the diversity of beliefs, particularly of the Gnostic variety, within early Christianity. John Dominic Crossan, another prominent and often provocative New Testament scholar, refers to these other early Christian gospels as "shadows on the contours of the canon."[19] Bart Ehrman's *Lost Scriptures* documents the plethora of writings by the diverse early Christian communities that never made it into the canon for a variety of reasons.[20] Scholarly biblical forums like

17. Luther, *Preface to Revelation*, 362.

18. Ehrman, *Lost Christianities*.

19. Dominic Crossan, *Four Other Gospels*.

20. Bart Ehrman, *Lost Scriptures*. While it is true that early Christianity produced a bewilderingly diverse array of writings, beliefs, and practices, it is not clear that all

Westar Institute, parent of the well-known (or notorious, depending on one's perspective) Jesus Seminar, are undertaking a reexamination of the canon, because they view our present canon as the product of the particular group within the early church that dominated the various doctrinal and political struggles and therefore imposed itself as "orthodoxy," thus relegating other early Christian movements to the status of "heresies."[21] In addition, following recent discoveries of long-lost and hitherto unknown Christian documents, such as *The Gospel of Thomas,* Westar has published its own "canon" of gospels that includes not only the Synoptics and John, but Thomas also (cf. *The Five Gospels,* Polebridge Press). Certain sects that claim to be Christian, yet are regarded as quasi-Christian heresies (e.g., the Latter-Day Saints or Mormons) by the more standard brands of Christianity, believe that the canon is open-ended with room for more inspired writings, such as those of Joseph Smith, to find their place within it. Other "canons" which are not the products of religious communities, such as the "canon" of great Western literature, are even more fluid, changing shape as ideological agendas, political pressures, or aesthetic tastes change. Scriptural canons, whether Christian or those of other religious traditions, are less dynamic than secular literary canons, but no canon is ever completely closed, the definitive decisions of the

---

of the writings that did not make it into the canon should be considered as "lost scriptures." Given the process of how writings become sacred scriptures described above, it is unlikely that many of these writings ever attained that status to begin with. Many of them were highly valued in very small, localized communities and were probably unknown in most other Christian communities. Lost they were, but whether they were ever "scriptures" is doubtful.

21 I must add my own personal rant here. While I was an associate fellow of the Westar Institute for some years, I do not support Westar's efforts to re-examine and urge change in the scriptural canon. The canon of the Christian scriptures is the product of the Christian church. It is the church's book in the most literal sense. While some of the scholars in Westar or other academic forums are practicing Christians, many are not. I do not regard it as a legitimate enterprise for a forum that is not rooted in the church to undertake to decide whether the church's book should be altered by inclusion or exclusion of certain texts. Only the church itself, in an evolutionary process such as that described above, can change its book. Imagine the furor that would result if the United Nations decided that it had the authority, not only to critique the U.S. Constitution, but to instruct the United States how it should alter the Constitution. Westar claims its rights on the basis that the Bible plays a larger role in Western culture than merely being the scriptures of the church, but this role is secondary. Only the church has a legitimate claim over the canon, and even that would be questioned by some Christians who believe the canon to be of divine origin. For better or worse, the question of the limits of the biblical canon is an "in-house" affair.

Council of Trent notwithstanding. Lectionaries may be seen as "canons within the canon" since they impose a selection of canonical readings for public worship. Since canons are both the product of communities and themselves shape succeeding communities, they are always, to a lesser or greater extent, open.

The process by which the canon (authoritative collection of scriptures) emerged was a complex and perfectly natural process. The historical forces at work both within and upon the early Christian communities were the chief influences on the eventual emergence of a defined list of scriptures. Real Christians in real congregations, worshiping, praying, working, evangelizing, suffering, studying, debating, defending their faith, and growing, gave us our Bible.

Chapter 5

A Tale Of Two Communities

Jews, Christians, and Their Scriptures

W alk into any Christian bookstore, or into the religion section of a large secular bookseller, and you will find many editions of a single volume that is most frequently titled, *The Holy Bible*. Some contemporary editions will have catchier names such as *The Message* or *The Living Bible* or *The Good News Bible* or even niche-editions like the *Life Application Study Bible* or *The Military Bible* (the latter comes in military green, with a simulated leather cover). Most of these are titles created by publishers to market the book to people who might not otherwise be attracted to the Christian scriptures.

The scriptures of Christianity did not always appear in this familiar and user-friendly form. The individual writings listed in the table of contents in our Bibles are not chapters in a single book. Rather, they are individual writings, penned by a variety of authors, written, rewritten, interwoven, edited, copied, and compiled over a time-period of approximately a thousand years, and were first united in a single collection sometime between the late-second and fourth centuries of the Common Era. The Bible is really an anthology of Jewish (and Jewish-Christian) religious writings rather than a single work. The act of collection and selection was the product of decisions, both formal and informal, made by real individuals and religious communities in a process that was the work of many centuries. The very title *The Holy Bible* attests to this: the word Bible is simply an English transliteration of the Greek word *biblos,* or "book," a description of the physical form in which the collected writings have been packaged. Prior to the production of the Christian scriptures, most writings, and the Jewish scriptures in particular, were done on parchment or vellum scrolls. At about the time Christian scribes were making copies of the writings of Christian authors, the codex was coming into fashion as a vehicle for written communication, and papyrus sheets a preferred surface for writing. A codex was the precursor of our modern book; it was a collection of papyrus or vellum sheets bound together between two covers. As a result of this new more convenient medium for collecting and transmitting documents, the Bible normally has been printed in book form, ever since. Jewish scribes still create Torah scrolls for use in synagogues, housed inside the "ark of the covenant" that is the central focus of liturgical space, and the scrolls are ceremoniously taken out for reading at the weekly Sabbath service. But scrolls are not convenient to carry around, and publishers also produce the Jewish versions of the Bible in modern book form as well. The term "holy" in the title *Holy Bible* distinguishes this book from other books. "Holy" means "set apart"; it distinguishes the scriptural writings contained between the covers from other writings because they are regarded as divinely inspired or, at least in some sense, authoritative or normative for the life and faith of people whose scriptures they are. The Christian Bible today is a combination of the Jewish scriptures that were "the Bible" of the earliest followers of Jesus plus the writings of some of those followers, themselves Jews, produced from the mid-first century CE to about the end of the first century or the very beginning of the second.

The founder figure around whom Christianity emerged was Jesus of Nazareth, an observant, if somewhat idiosyncratic, Jewish man probably born in or around the town of Nazareth in Galilee, near the lake that is often called the Sea of Galilee. At the time of his birth, the region was under the last years of the reign of Herod the Great, a local king of the Idumaean people who had previously embraced Jewish religion. Herod had been educated as a child in Rome, and later returned to Palestine to rule over it as Rome's proxy. Jesus appears to have been very devout, something of a visionary and prophet, was addressed as rabbi (teacher) by the group of followers he attracted, virtually all of them Jewish as well from the peasant and artisan classes of the surrounding area. For a period of one to three years (scholars disagree on the exact length of time), Jesus and his followers, some of whom were women (one fact that warrants the description "idiosyncratic") appear to have itinerated through the countryside, proclaiming the imminent arrival of something he called "the kingdom of God," or "God's imperial rule." In fact, he may well have believed that this new social/political/religious reality was actually coming into view in the movement he inspired, and was a sign of God's imminent consummation of human history, though not all scholars are in agreement on this point. The parables and stories about Jesus and the movement that arose around him have come down to us in a series of writings that were given the name Gospels (an old English translation of the Greek word *euanggélion*, which means "good news," and from which we get our English terms "evangelist" and "evangelical"). The Gospel writers are often referred to as "the Four Evangelists."

The Gospels were written several decades after Jesus' death following a period of forty to sixty years during which the stories about him and sayings or teachings attributed to him were primarily transmitted orally. Many of the common people in that era were still illiterate, and so information was passed on by word of mouth, by telling stories. The authors of the Gospels were people with some degree of education, who were not actually among Jesus' personal entourage, since the earliest of the Gospels (Mark) didn't appear until sometime around 70 CE. It may have been the death or approaching death of the last of Jesus' original followers and/or the cataclysm that overtook Judea with the destruction of Jerusalem in 70 CE, by the Roman general Titus, that prompted the process of committing the oral tradition to writing. It is likely that the writers of the Gospels were leaders in their respective faith communities, and sometimes, by careful use of the critical tools described in an earlier chapter, we can catch glimpses of the issues and questions confronting those communities which the Gospel writers were attempting to address. Though there are many variations of the stories and sayings attributed to Jesus in the canonical Gospels (including a number of somewhat later gospels that never made it into the Bible), they do give us enough information about Jesus to draw a fairly reliable, if sketchy, portrait.[1]

1. The extent to which the stories in the Christian Gospels are based on events or sources with a high degree of historical probability is a question that has occupied biblical scholars for more than two hundred years. Three "quests" for the "historical Jesus" have resulted in much new information about the social, political, and religious context of Jesus' life and ministry as well as some fairly assured results authenticating some of the sayings and actions attributed to him. However, there is also much about him, particularly about his own self-consciousness, that remains uncertain. That he proclaimed a "kingdom of God" characterized by just and loving economic and social relationships, as well as prophetic opposition to the status quo of institutionalized Jewish religion as it manifested itself in the Temple cult in Jerusalem, is highly probable. That so much about "the historical Jesus" remains uncertain may be seen simply by the astonishing variety of portraits of him produced by the questers of the past two centuries since the modern historical investigations of the New Testament began.

Since Jesus and his followers were Jews, they inherited a tradition of understanding and interpretation from their own cultural and religious past, and particularly the scriptures of Israel, which are commonly referred to in Christian circles as the Old Testament.[2] The meanings or interpretations produced by these centuries of writing, reading, and reflection prior to Jesus' time were part of the cultural and religious landscape of the earliest Christians, just as the Analects of Confucius are part of the cultural landscape of most Chinese people, or the Declaration of Independence, the U.S. Constitution, the story of the first Thanksgiving, and Lincoln's Gettysburg Address are part of the cultural landscape of most Americans. Any people's cultural and religious landscape, which is firmly wedded to language, forms the backdrop against which all thought and understanding of reality takes place within that culture. It provides the raw material for thought, meaning, and worldview. In what follows, for convenience, whenever I use the term "landscape," I mean the whole complex of images, values, customs, vocabulary, rituals, symbols, and commonly shared understandings, including religion, that make up a culture. It is that "landscape," often not consciously perceived, that forms the matrix that individuals and groups draw upon when reflecting on their experiences. Or, to use a different metaphor, culture is the pair of spectacles *through* which we look at

> **Side Track: O Say, Can You See?**
>
> Imagine two people, one an American and one a Tibetan Buddhist monk, reading the phrase "the star-spangled banner," and then being asked what meaning that phrase has for them. What effect will differences in their respective "cultural and religious landscapes" have on their answers? Suppose, further, that our imaginary American and Tibetan are standing side-by-side when the American national anthem is played by a band. How might each react? What differences in their responses would be attributable to the differences in their respective cultural "landscapes"?

2. The term "Old Testament (or Covenant)" is a Christian name for the scriptures they inherited from their Jewish religious tradition and which were composed well before the time of Jesus. It is an interpretive term first given to these writings by the Christians of the late second and third centuries CE when Christians saw themselves in relation to Jews as possessors of a separate and superior religion. The "old" in "Old Testament" was (and remains for some) an implicit interpretation of Christianity's relationship to Judaism; it located Christianity with respect to Judaism and assigned a value both to Judaism and to itself. "Old" in the sense Christians have historically used the word, does not simply mean "earlier in time" or "ancient" but also "that which has been superceded" and in consequence, of less value as well. In more recent years, the term has lost some of that value-judgment quality and has become simply a term of convenience to simplify which part of the Bible one is talking about.

the world, though we only occasionally look *at* the spectacles themselves, usually when there's a smudge that needs to be cleaned.

Some Christian scholars have advocated the use of the term "Hebrew Scriptures" or "First Testament" instead of "Old Testament" because they reject the longstanding notion that Christianity has superceded Judaism (see note 2). The term "Hebrew Scriptures" accords the scriptures of Judaism their own integrity within their own religious and historical context. Not all Christians agree with this perspective, however, and many sincerely hold to the historic view that Christianity has indeed superceded Judaism as the definitive recipient of God's revelation. Many Jewish scholars themselves are as uncomfortable with the term "Hebrew Scriptures" or "First Testament" as they are with "Old Testament" since both are Christian designations of the Jewish scriptures, and both are theological and ideologically-driven terms.

Judaism simply refers to its scriptures collectively either as Tanak, or simply "scriptures." Tanak is an acronym composed of the three consonants T, N, and K which are the first letters of the Hebrew words for the three categories by which Jews organize their scriptures: *Torah* (Law), *Nebi'im* (Prophets), and *Kethubim* (Writings). Because of the centrality of the Torah for Judaism, some Jews simply use the term Torah as a shorthand way of referring to all the scriptures.

Within Judaism, the scriptures have both similar and very different meanings than they do within Christianity. Jews differ as greatly in their attitude toward the scriptures as do Christians, with some very orthodox groups believing that every "jot and tittle" of the text is literally God-breathed or inspired. Others take a much more liberal or nuanced approach, believing that they are primarily writings that record the foundational narratives of their people, particularly their story in relationship to the God who revealed himself to their primal ancestor Abraham. Regardless of differences in belief regarding the origin and nature of the scriptures, Judaism has always maintained a strong tradition of encouraging multiple interpretations of scriptural texts. An old rabbinic tradition that every scripture is susceptible to at least seventy different interpretations is typical of Jewish approaches to these texts.

The three-fold division of the Jewish scriptures may be envisioned as three concentric circles. Torah is the innermost circle, telling the fundamental story of Israel's origins, its understanding of its election by God, the defining event of the Exodus and the giving of God's law to Moses at Sinai, and the subsequent conquest and settlement of "the promised land" of Canaan. The second circle, the Prophets, expands that story into the period of the monarchy, and serves as a critical commentary on the faithfulness or lack of it, of the kingdoms of Israel and later Judah, as well as God's providential care for the people. The outer circle, the Writings, contains a wide-ranging collection of material—court histories, folk tales, liturgical psalms and poetry, philosophical "wisdom," erotic poems, etc.—covering various aspects of Israel's life and worship.

The Torah, which includes the first five books of the Bible, is attributed to Moses the great Lawgiver, and is said to have been divinely given to Moses on Mount Sinai, with its synopsis, the Ten Commandments, written by God on tablets of stone. The Torah is accorded the highest value in the Tanak. Several stories about the giving of the Torah to Moses, found in the teachings of ancient rabbis, demonstrate the degree of sacredness with which the Torah is regarded. One such story, widely taught, was that the original Torah was revealed simultaneously in all the known languages (70 was the number thought to exist) of the world, but that only the Jews were willing to accept it. This tradition may lie behind the story in the New Testament Book of Acts where we find a list of all the "tongues" or "languages" in which the audience heard the apostles speaking on the Day of Pentecost. Even today, in Jewish worship services, the sacredness of the Torah is emphasized by the fact that it is read only (or at least first) in Hebrew, even though most of the congregation may not understand the language.

The Prophets record, not only the dynastic histories and genealogies of Israel, but the warnings spoken and written by prophets who were understood as spokesmen for God to recall God's people and their kings from error, back to the way of obedience to Torah. Always God's faithfulness to the chosen people is either implicit or explicit in the Prophets. The Prophets are divided into two groups: the Former Prophets (*Joshua, Judges, Samuel, Kings*), and the Latter Prophets (*Isaiah, Jeremiah, Ezekiel,* and *The Book of the Twelve*—what Christians call the Minor Prophets—*Hosea, Joel, Amos, Obadiah, Jonah, Micah, Nahum, Habbakuk, Zephaniah, Haggai, Zechariah, Malachi*).

The Writings contain an assortment of writings ranging from liturgical material (*Psalms*) to literature from various sub-movements or literary genres within Judaism such as "Wisdom" (*Job, Proverbs, Ecclesiastes*) or "apocalyptic" (*Daniel*), court histories and genealogical tables (*Chronicles*), parables (*Jonah*), and even romantic morality tales (*Ruth*) and erotic poetry (*Song of Songs*).

At the time of the beginnings of Christianity, the scriptures of Judaism included the same writings that Protestants now accept as the Old Testament. These scriptures were written in Hebrew, which, at the time of Jesus, was already a "dead" language, i.e., it was not spoken as the common language of any group of people, but was known only by scholars, much as Latin is known today. The common spoken languages of Palestine in Jesus' time were Aramaic and Greek (Aramaic was the court language of the former Persian Empire, and had been spread widely among its vassal nations prior to Alexander the Great's conquest when Greek began to replace it). Aramaic was almost certainly Jesus' mother-tongue, and he may have been more or less versatile with "marketplace Greek" as well, particularly in Galilee, a strongly Greek-oriented region. The Jewish "canon" or the authoritative list of writings had not yet been formally selected, and would not be until well into the Christian era. In fact, it was probably the emergence and popularity of Christian writings, some of which later became the New Testament, that motivated Jews to formulate their own authorized list of writings considered to be sacred scripture.

Although the Christian Bible emerged from and included the scriptures of Judaism, the written scriptures do not play the same role or serve the same functions in Judaism as they do in Christianity. Judaism has always considered the Written Teaching (Torah) to be one of two equal sources of authority. The other, the Halakah, is a collection of oral interpretations of the Torah, traditionally considered by some Jews to have been revealed to Moses simultaneously with the written Torah on Mount Sinai. This oral law, passed on from rabbi to students for generations, was collected and compiled in written form in the Mishna and Talmuds around the third century CE. The Prophets and the Writings, while valuable and certainly part of the Jewish Bible, have never been considered to have the same revelatory authority as either the Torah or the Halakah. Islam has a similar collection of *hadith*, the oral teachings of the Prophet Muhammad, which are also accorded great authority, only slightly less than that of the Qu'ran. Christianity, however, while it has purported sayings of Jesus from the period of the oral tradition contained in the Gospels, has, at least from the third century onward, moved away from a concept of "oral law" or "oral scriptures." While the oral tradition was valued more highly than written testimonies at least into the second century, Christian scriptural authority has mostly been centered in written texts. Christianity arose at a pivotal point of human linguistic and cultural change—the shift from orality to literacy as a primary means of

transmission of informa-
tion and cultural values. To
a large extent this may have
been the product of the
Hellenization that followed
Alexander's conquests. The
Greeks appear to have been
among the first people to
discover that language and
culture can be deliberately
transmitted through formal
teaching; hence, the rise of
schools.

The Jewish scriptures
that existed in Hebrew manuscripts contained the same
writings as current Prot-
estant versions of the Old
Testament, albeit in the different groupings and order
described above. The Sep-
tuagint (third-century BCE
Greek translation of Hebrew
scriptures) included other
writings which have come to
be commonly known as the
Apocrypha. They were eventually excluded from the
Jewish canon, though they
continued to be accepted
by some segments of the
Jewish community, particularly the more Hellenized
segments, and also by most
Christians until the time of
the Protestant Reformation.
It was this Greek translation of the Jewish scriptures,

Side Track: "Born of a Virgin"

As the earliest Christians read their Bibles—the Jewish
scriptures— they read them in the Greek version, the
Septuagint. The Septuagint's translation of Isaiah 7:14
rendered the Hebrew word *almah*, which means "young
woman" or "girl," by the Greek term *parthénos* which
means "virgin" or "chaste woman" (or "chaste man" in its
masculine form). In addition, another piece of "cultural
furniture" in the Hellenistic world was the relatively common practice of attributing the greatness of an extraor-
dinary human being to a union between that person's
mother or father and a god or goddess. Alexander the
Great's accomplishments were explained in this way, as
were those of Augustus.

Early Christians needed to explain the significance
of Jesus to Gentiles attracted to the movement that grew
from their preaching about his resurrection. Their reading of the Greek translation of Isaiah 7:14 combined with
their reinterpretation of other prophetic writings in light
of their experience of Jesus, led inevitably to the notion
that Jesus was the Son of God, not only in the Jewish sense
of messiah or Anointed One, but also in the Hellenistic
sense of a great man with semi-divine parentage. That this
happened relatively early is indisputable; St. Paul, whose
writings are the earliest in the New Testament, appears
to know nothing about any "virgin birth," and in fact even
disparages the importance of Jesus' historical life before
his resurrection. (Cf. 2 Corinthians 5:16— "Even if we once
knew the Messiah according to the flesh, we do not know
him that way any longer.") Yet, by the time Matthew and
Luke wrote their Gospels, approximately 50–60 years after
Jesus' crucifixion, they clearly tell a story of Jesus' virgin
birth, that is similar, in substance if not in detail, to other
such stories of the birth of certain heroes or great men
in the Hellenistic world. Their conviction that God had
raised Jesus from death also strengthened their argument
that he must have had an equally special birth. By the third
century, in some quarters of the church, particularly in the
East, Mary began to be hailed as *theotokos*, the God-bearer,
or Mother of God—a title formally bestowed by the Council of Ephesus in 431 CE.

the Septuagint, that was the "Bible" of the earliest followers of Jesus, at least those who could read. Almost all of the quotations from the Old Testament that appear in the New Testament are quotations from the Septuagint.

Today, however, the Apocrypha aside, Jews, Protestants, Roman Catholics, and Eastern Orthodox Christians all hold a library of sacred writings in common—what we commonly call the Old Testament, though the significance and meanings of some those writings are understood very differently by Jews and Christians.

New Religion, New Bible

When the earliest Christians, probably motivated by a desire to make sense of Jesus' brutal crucifixion by the Roman occupation authorities, began to reflect upon their experience of having met and followed Jesus, their religious "landscape" provided them with two primary images for identifying and describing his significance for them. These were the images of the son of God and messiah. In the Old Testament, the phrase "son(s) of God" is used to speak of 1) heavenly or angelic beings (cf. Pss 29:1; 82:6; Job 1:6, 2:1; Gen 1:26, 3:22); 2) Israel as a whole (cf. Deut 14:1, 32:5–6; Isa 43:6–7; Jer 2:27); and 3) the king as God's anointed ruler (cf. Pss 2:7, 89:19–37, 110:3; 2 Sam 7:14). Before the Christian era, there is no evidence that the term "son of God" was conferred as a title upon a Davidic ruler by Jews with messianic hopes. Yet, when Christians began to reflect on the meaning of Jesus, this image was part of their "mental furniture" or "landscape," and thus suggested itself as a designation appropriate to their experience with Jesus. Even then, it was not immediately applied to Jesus during his historical ministry. In Paul's letters, which are the earliest in our New Testament, "son(s) of God" is primarily a description of the status of Christians themselves in the new age that has been ushered in by the resurrection of Jesus, who himself was "appointed a son of God in power by virtue of a spirit of holiness, as a result of resurrection from the dead" (Rom 1:4, my translation). For Paul, in other words, the designation "son of God" was conferred by God upon Jesus *after* his death, and that this conferral was tied both to Jesus' own exemplary life of faithfulness to God and to God's action in raising him from the dead. By the time of the Gospels one or two decades later, this designation is beginning to be applied to Jesus in his historical existence (cf. Mark 1:1), but not exclusively so; Jesus, rather, is the firstborn of all those who are now "sons of God" under the new covenant.

The second image, messiah, was probably one that was prominent in the minds of the earliest followers of Jesus of Nazareth during his public ministry. The term itself simply means "anointed one" (Greek translation: *christos,* from which we get the English "Christ"), and in the Jewish scriptures was never used to speak of a divine redeemer figure or savior in the future. Though the history of this term and the concepts associated with it are beyond the scope of this study, the most common Old Testament usage of the term is as a reference to the anointed king, though these are not numerous. With the exception of Habakkuk 3:13, where the term refers explicitly to the king, and Isaiah 45:1, where it is Cyrus the Persian emperor who is termed by God "my anointed," the actual term *messiah* never appears elsewhere in the prophetic writings. In the prophets, there are oracles that speak of a future Davidic king who will fulfill the ideal of kingship that none of Israel's historical kings, including David himself, ever did, in some future utopian age. These oracles gradually evolved into the expectation of the coming of a divine savior figure in some circles of Judaism in the first and second centuries before Jesus. Some of the Dead Sea scrolls and such Jewish/Christian writings such as the Sibylline Oracles, show a definite progression toward a belief in a heavenly redeemer who descends to earth to establish a reign of righteousness, though some of these oracles are later than our New Testament, and may have been influenced by the early Christian proclamations about Jesus.[3]

Certain segments of the Jewish community in Palestine at the time of Jesus were so disillusioned with the present state of the world that they saw the world as incorrigibly wicked and beyond redemption. They expected God to bring an end to history and usher in a new age of righteousness. These people, who were deeply pessimistic about the present course of the world and their own situation in particular, expected a messiah or "anointed one" to come and inaugurate this new age, though how the messiah would come, or who it would be, or what would happen when the messiah came was hotly debated and not at all clear. Certainly the first Jewish war of rebellion against Rome, which broke out in 63 CE and brought on the catastrophe of Jerusalem's destruction in 70

---

3. Richard Rubenstein's *When Jesus Became God*, Philip Jenkins's *Jesus Wars*, and Charles Freeman's *A New History of Early Christianity*, are readable accounts of the struggles within the first six centuries of the church's existence over how to understand Jesus.

CE, including the destruction of the Temple, fanned the flames of this apocalyptic strain of thought. One of the apocryphal Jewish writings, the Apocalypse of Baruch, roughly contemporary with the Gospel of Mark (which itself reflects the same catastrophic events, cf. Mark 13), claims that when the Messiah comes, "on one vine will be a thousand branches, and one branch will produce a thousand clusters, and one cluster will produce a thousand grapes, and one grape will produce a cor (56 liters) of wine." (The wine producers would be devastated by the impact on prices of such an oversupply, although the consumers would probably be too happy to notice!) The circles within Judaism espousing such ideas generated writings of their own that have come to be known as apocalyptic literature or simply apocalypses. This term refers not only to the particular literary genre of the writings, but to the mood or worldview espoused by these particular Jews—a mood characterized by social alienation from the "powers that be" and a loss of hope of betterment arising from current political action or historical trends. Apocalyptic hope is projected beyond history to the Future Blessed Age or the world to come; or if I may state it more crudely, hope for "pie in the sky by-and-by."

By no means, however, were all Jews "messianic," i.e., looking for a deliverance from present turmoil or suffering by an "anointed one" (messiah), nor did apocalyptic alienation and "end of the world" expectation characterize all Jewish religion and sentiment. In fact, it appears that those segments of first-century Judaism that were messianic were a distinct minority. It was disagreement on this very issue that separated the earliest followers of Jesus from their fellow Jews. In such passages as Acts 9:22 and 18:5, Luke presents Paul as arguing in the synagogues that Jesus is *ho christos,* the Messiah expected by some within the Jewish religious community. The response was mixed, though predominantly negative among Paul's Jewish hearers, which, according to his own complicated argument in Romans 9–11, is the reason he embraced the positive response of the non-Jews to his proclamation. It was among the culturally Greek Christians, whether of Jewish or Gentile descent, that the notion of a divine redeemer figure who comes to earth to save the world began to play an increasingly important part, since it was already part of the cultural landscape of the Hellenistic world.

The destruction of Jerusalem and the Temple and its cult of sacrifice and ritual was one factor that began to move first-century Jewish religion in the direction of having not only a collection of *authoritative scriptures,* but an *authoritative collection* of scriptures. The war also revealed deep divisions within the population of Judea and in Jewish religious life. Some sects or parties, e.g., the priestly aristocracy in Jerusalem, favored cooperation with Roman over-lordship in order to have peace, prosperity, and a measure of autonomy in both the practice of their religion and in local governance. Others, inflamed by nationalist or religious sentiment, e.g., the Zealots, found such cooperation intolerable, even treasonous, and advocated continued armed insurrection. Still others, e.g., some of the Pharisees, took diverse approaches, ranging from the renewed concentration on quietly studying and devoutly practicing the commands of the Torah to fervently embracing apocalyptic hopes for the imminent coming of a divinely appointed liberator or messiah to end history and usher in a paradisal future. Much of early Christianity originated within that particular apocalyptic or messianic strain within first-century Jewish religion. Those embracing the apocalyptic strain tended to see the Roman conquest of the Holy City as the precursor of the imminent "end of the world" and the "appearing" (*parousia*) of the messiah to inaugurate the Future Blessed Age. Many, if not most, Jews, however, saw the destruction of Jerusalem as a decisive defeat and the discrediting of apocalyptic movements and hopes, whether of the violent Zealot-type or the less violent apocalypticism of the Jesus movement. Some in the Jesus movement and others within the larger Jewish community continued to espouse such hopes, and continued to produce writings that reflected their point of view (e.g., Jude, Revelation, 4th Ezra, Apocalypse of Baruch). As these writings gained credence in some circles, in others, a move began to more clearly delimit which writings would have normative authority, over against such sectarian perspectives.

Yochanan ben Zakkai, a prominent Pharisaic rabbi, appears to have been particularly influential, both in the delimitation of the writings accepted as scripture and in leading a shift away from apocalypticism toward a form of Jewish life and religious practice centered on the study of Torah. He applied to the Romans for permission to withdraw from Jerusalem to Jamnia (modern-day Javneh in Gaza) and devote himself along with his students and colleagues to the study of Torah. The Romans gave permission, perhaps because ben Zakkai was able to convince them that no further messianic movements would arise out of his group to disturb the peace and inflame nationalistic passions. (Christianity also diversified beyond its apocalyptic roots in the period after 70 CE, particularly as increasing numbers of Jews from the diaspora and Gentiles joined "the Way," as early Jesus-followers were known.)

The internal struggle between competing sectarian movements within the broad stream of Jewish life in Palestine had been going on since before the time of Jesus. The Jesus movement was just one tributary within the broader, quite varied stream of Jewish cultural and religious life, but the tensions between it and the others, already present prior to the catastrophe of 70 CE, reached a breaking point sometime between 80 and 90 CE. Then Christianity began to take on the characteristics of a separate religion, increasingly so as Gentiles began to respond to Christian preaching in large numbers and local congregations of Jesus-followers were established.

The evidence of this intra-Jewish family feud has echoes everywhere in the Christian writings that became the New Testament. In some of Paul's writings (e.g., Galatians), the polemic appears to be directed against Jews (who are also presumably followers of Jesus) who insist that it is incumbent on Jewish Jesus-followers to remain faithful to the Law of Moses, particularly in dietary matters and sexual morality. The negative and often hostile characterizations of "the Jews" in the Gospel of John or "scribes and Pharisees, hypocrites" in the Gospel of Matthew or the Pharisees' accusations against Jesus in the Gospel of Mark that he gains his healing powers from Beelzebul ("Lord of the Flies")—an extremely hostile and scatological epithet—also reflect the intensity of this "family feud."

To the best of our knowledge, all the New Testament authors were Jews. In the period of time when Paul's epistles and the Gospels were being written, all their original readers would have known that the hostile language in those writings was directed against other Jews, specifically both opponents of the Jesus movement who thought it heretical, and also other Jewish followers of Jesus who insisted that keeping the Law of Moses was still necessary and that Gentile converts had to be observant. Elaine Pagels, in her recent book *Revelations: Visions, Prophecy, and Politics in the Book of Revelation*, makes a credible argument that some of the polemic in that book is aimed, not only at Rome, but at other Jewish Christians who advocated laxity with respect to the Mosaic law.[4] However, regrettably, and often fatally, later generations of (now predominantly) Gentile readers of the New Testament were ignorant of this old intra-Jewish family feud, and interpreted the hostile language as directed against all Jews. Rather than being understood as

4. Elaine Pagels, *Revelations*.

"us faithful Jews against those unfaithful Jews," it tragically became "us faithful Christians against those infidel Jews." Thus began the historically and morally disastrous rise of Christian anti-Semitism

Though we cannot be certain that ben Zakkai, and his circle of rabbis and students at Jamnia about 90 CE, actually decided the issues of which scriptures or writings measured up or didn't, we do know that after that date, there is little further discussion in Jewish circles about which writings were authoritative and which weren't. The Jewish canon was now, for all intents and purposes, complete, and it did not include any writings produced by authors who were followers of "The Way," the earliest known designation of Jesus-followers. This is evidence in itself that the community of Judaism[5] was defining itself over against the fledgling Jesus movement, and delimiting its scriptures to the *de facto* canon that already existed at the time of Jesus. After Jamnia, what Jews call Tanak (*Torah, Nebiim, Kethubim*) and Christians call the Old Testament now existed as an entity complete in itself, recognized by two communities as such, and used by them in sometimes similar, but often very different ways. We will look next at the way in which the Christians made use of this Jewish canon to define themselves over against other forms of Judaism, and developed their own canon that included and went beyond the canon of Judaism.

Jesus' crucifixion must have dealt a crushing blow to the hopes of many of his followers, particularly those who had seen him as the Messiah. The Messiah wasn't supposed to suffer defeat. But though he met a brutal end, at least some of them became convinced that through God's power, he had somehow triumphed over death. It is difficult to say whether it was their reading and searching of their scriptures to find meaning in the face of Jesus' crucifixion that led them to the conviction that he was alive, and hence to the accounts of their encounters with the risen Jesus, or whether it was the visionary or ecstatic experience of meeting Jesus alive that drove them back into their scriptures to try to find a way to explain the unexplainable. Whatever the sequence, the fact is that those earliest Christians, and in particular, the apostle Paul, used the language of their own Jewish cultural and religious tradition, particularly the Pharisaic and apocalyptic strains, to describe what they believed had happened to Jesus of Nazareth as "resurrection from the dead." In this sense, the

5. The term "Judaism" as applied to first century Jewish religion and culture is something of an anachronism. Jewish religion was not nearly as unified or monolithic as the term implies. I use it here purely as a term of convenience.

resurrection may be termed a "language-event"; that is, the question of what happened cannot be separated from the language in which it is described or imaged. It could also be described as a "biblical" or "scriptural" event in this same way, because it can only be understood or imagined with reference to particular language in particular writings—the Jewish scriptures which provided the vocabulary, images, and symbols for the earliest Christians.

In other words, the notion of resurrection is not a Christian invention. A few hundred years before the Christian era, some Jews had begun to develop a belief in resurrection from the dead. Though only in Isaiah 26:19 and Daniel 12:13 among the "canonical" books of the Hebrew scriptures is there an explicit reference to resurrection, other passages were used to bolster this notion, e.g., Psalm 103:4; Job 19:25–26; 33:18; 33:30, et al. The concept of resurrection may have been appropriated from Persian religious thought during the Exile in the sisth and fifth centuries BCE, since no specific mention or even hint of such a concept appears in Jewish writings prior to the Exile. By the time of Jesus, the Pharisees, among others, already believed in resurrection from the dead, which they conceived as something God would do for all the righteous dead at the end of history.[6] So the earliest followers

> **Side Track: Other Landscapes**
>
> 1) What other "prophecies" of Jesus can you think of in the Old Testament? (E.g., read Isaiah 7:1–18 and 8:11—9:7.) If you were a faithful Jew who lived prior to Jesus, how might you have read these oracles? Then consider how these oracles, particularly 7:14 and 9:6–7, became more or less mandatory for Christian liturgical use during Advent and Christmas.
>
> 2) Imagine, if you can, that Jesus had been an Indian Hindu guru during the time of the Mughal empire instead of a Galilean Jew. If his followers (also Hindu) had seen their leader brutally executed by their Mughal overlords, how might they have interpreted or given meaning to that death? What would the difference in their language and/or their scriptures make in both the way they described it and the meaning they attached to it?

6. Recently, Kevin Madigan and Jon Levenson, in their book *Resurrection*, have convincingly argued that the notion of resurrection in Judaism is a logical, evolutionary development of Jewish theology, and is not only focused on the survival of individuals beyond death, but on the restoration of social justice in the world. Ironically, while many mainline Protestants who have traditionally been strong advocates for social justice have simply given up on any belief in the resurrection, many evangelical Protestants, for whom the resurrection had been primarily about the individual's destination after death, have have now begun to see its implications for a just society in this world.

of Jesus who believed in his resurrection were not inventing something for which no language or images existed. Their own scriptures (as well as apocryphal books such as 4 Maccabees) reread in light of their experience, provided them with language which helped them interpret or give meaning to that experience. And that discovery, in turn, sent them back to their scriptures, this time equipped with the new lens of their faith in the resurrection of Jesus the messiah, to read and reread everything through that lens. In hundreds of passages in the Hebrew scriptures which had very specific meanings to the people for whom they were written and by whom they were written, the Christians now found new meanings—to them, everything pointed to Christ (messiah). Even Jesus' crucifixion, which completely discredited both Jesus and his followers in the eyes of many Jews and Greeks (cf. 1 Cor 1:18–25), now took on new meaning. The transformation of the "servant songs" of Isaiah into prophecies of Jesus' passion and death, which we looked at earlier, is but one of many examples.

As Christians appropriated the "Servant Songs" and the "Passion Psalms" to interpret Jesus' crucifixion, so too, did early Christian testimonies to Jesus' resurrection use images reconfigured from the scriptures of Israel. In fact, it is not too far from the mark to claim, as some have, that the New Testament is simply an imaginative reinterpretation of the Old in light of the fledgling church's experience of God in the person of Jesus of Nazareth.

Luke's story in the Book of Acts (ch. 17) about Paul preaching to the philosophers in Athens on Mars Hill illustrates something of the difficulty posed in trying to communicate meaning in a different cultural and linguistic landscape. To the Athenian philosophers, whose culture and language did not have a concept of resurrection from the dead, Paul's words seemed nonsensical, and they wrote him off as a lunatic.

The earliest Jewish Christians, while rooted in their own religious tradition and language, were also citizens of a world heavily dominated by Hellenistic culture, in much the same way as many cultures today have become "Americanized" through the world-wide marketing of products like Coca-Cola or Hollywood movies or MacDonald's and Starbucks. To the extent that they were Hellenized, all of them were possessed of the various "mental furnishings" or "lenses" of that culture which provided them with a huge variety of images or concepts with which to explore the meaning of their experiences with Jesus. As Gentiles came to follow the new faith in ever-increasing numbers, these Hellenistic images became even more important than the ones drawn from Judaism or were used to reinterpret them in new ways. The early Christian reinterpretation of the Jewish scriptures in a Christocentric way led inevitably to the self-understanding of many Christians that they were the true heirs of God's covenants with Israel. While Paul agonized over the role that Israel still played within God's redemptive purposes, and concluded that God's covenant with Israel remained valid and in force (cf. Romans 9–11), by the time the Gospels of Matthew and Luke were written, this was no longer the case. Matthew appears to argue for the church as the *new* Israel with Jesus as the "new Moses" who gives a "new Law" (the Sermon on the Mount). Luke, on the other hand, argues for the church as the *true* Israel, perhaps in an attempt to get official Roman recognition for Christianity as a legitimate religion similar to, but distinct from and superseding, Judaism. In Luke's perspective, Christianity inherited the promises made by God to Israel and succeeded Israel as the true (and exclusive) people of God. While Luke's arguments may not have convinced the Roman state of Christianity's status, they did convince enough other Christians that the whole edifice of later Christian attitudes of superiority to Judaism— often called the doctrine of supersessionism—was built upon them.

One prominent churchman and biblical scholar, the late Krister Stendahl, has written about this notion of Christianity as something that supersedes Judaism as one of two possible roads the early Church might have taken. One road would have been to see a common "shape" to God's ways with the world, to see an analogy between Passover and Easter, between Mount Moriah and Golgotha, between the giving of the Law on Sinai and the Sermon on the Mount—in effect, making Christianity a "Judaism for Gentiles."[7] However, he laments, this was "the road not taken." Instead, Judaism and Christianity became two rival schools of biblical interpretation, competing with one another over the right to authoritatively interpret the scriptures of Israel. Instead of Israel's faith being extended to the Gentiles through the gracious action of God in raising the faithful Jew, Jesus of Nazareth, from the dead, the world got the whole depressing history of struggle and animosity between the two communities, sadly dominated by Christian anti-Semitism.

"There is Abel over Cain, Isaac over Ishmael, Jacob over Esau, Joseph over his older brothers, Israel over Canaan—and the pattern continues, not only Church over Synagogue, but Islam over both Judaism and

7. Krister Stendahl, "Qumran and Supercessionism," 136.

Christianity, and Protestants over Catholics in the Reformation. In no case is complementarity or coexistence an option chosen; there is always the claim to exclusive legitimacy."[8]

This tendency of Christians to claim the right of inheritance and authoritative interpretation of the Jewish scriptures, and the history of anti-Semitism it has engendered through the centuries, has led another contemporary biblical scholar Burton Mack to label the Nazi Holocaust as "a Gospel event."[9] By this, he means that the harsh language in the gospels, which originally reflected the internal struggle within Judaism between Jews who believed in Jesus as messiah and those who didn't, was misread by later Gentile Christians, who were ignorant of the original context. Such misreadings, interpreting such language as directed against all Jews, became the "biblical" foundation used to justify Christian perse-cution of Jews. Few would be likely to agree with Mack's conclusions that in view of the long and dishonorable history of Christian anti-Semitism, we ought to simply throw out the Gospels.

However, his and Stendahl's work, along with James Carroll's more recent best-seller *Constantine's Sword*,[10] should at least sensitize us to the fact that reading the Bible through certain lenses or with certain areas of ignorance has been responsible for a persistent, devastating, and reprehensible treatment of Jews by Christians, particularly in the European nations that were once part of Christendom. Given this sad history, it might be safer to adopt a certain humility, realizing that what we see of God's will, God's intent, and God's nature at any given point in time is limited to *what is visible from our angle,* and that there may be other angles from which the same things may be viewed, including, and perhaps especially, the texts that function as sacred scriptures for both religious communities.

---

8. Ibid., 137.

9. Burton Mack, *A Myth of Innocence*, 375.

10. James Carroll, *Constantine's Sword*.

Chapter 6

Human Words, God's Word

W e are now reaching the end of our quest to discover what is involved when we or anyone else makes the claim "The Bible
says. . ." or "The Bible teaches. . ." The quest was motivated by the conflicts
within religious institutions and the larger society over a wide variety of
controversial issues that have cultural, ethical, and theological dimensions: whether homosexuals or transgendered persons may marry or be
ordained to ministry, the role of women in marriage and church life, and
Christian participation in war, to name only a few. In all these conflicts,
there are persons holding opposite points of view who claim that the
Bible sanctions their position. In their minds, at least, that claim gives
strength or even finality to their arguments. We began this study with
some observations about implicit or explicit assumptions in the minds
of those who make such a claim. Those assumptions raised some critical
questions that have guided our discussions: What is the Bible? What role
does (or should) it play in authorizing the views of those who accord it
authority on a variety of issues? Who has the right or responsibility to
interpret the Bible, i.e., to say what it says and what it means by what it
says? Who guarantees that right will be exercised responsibly? What does
"responsible exercise" mean in any given instance, especially when diametrically opposing conclusions are drawn? What *does* it mean to make
the claim, "The Bible says. . .?"

One goal of this study has been to construct an understanding of
what the Bible really is by looking at the Bible's own history as a collection
of writings that has been produced by, and which has produced in turn,
living communities of faith for whom the Bible is sacred. Rather than beginning with a "confession" of belief about the Bible that often takes little

or no account of the Bible as the product of a historical process, nor with a critical approach that sometimes is content with historical excavation, or worse, in some cases, actually fosters a "debunking" agenda, I have advocated an understanding of the Bible as the collection of writings that emerge from, and bear witness to, living human communities in their encounters with life's "root experiences" or "ultimate concerns" or the "transcendent." This journey has taken us through a look at human culture and language, and to the realization that we can say nothing about the Bible or about anything else, for that matter, that does not arise out of our embeddedness in a particular cultural and linguistic setting. We are "languaged" beings; language is necessary for thought and is inseparable from the specific cultural/social/religious "landscape" into which we are born and in which we are nurtured.

We have followed the emergence of our biblical writings from the culture of ancient Israel, and have traced their evolution and development as they became "holy scripture," both for Israel and later for the early Christians. We have seen how writings become scriptures, and how scriptures become canonical, i.e., explicitly or implicitly authorized by a living community of faith as that which grounds the life of that community through time. And we have looked at some of the ways in which those authorized writings have shaped the communities that authorized them and the ways in which those communities shaped the writings by the processes of selection, ordering, and interpreting. Specifically, we focused on the ways the earliest Christian communities shaped and were shaped by the scriptures of Israel, so that they bridged the gap between the history of Israel and the (predominantly) non-Jewish, Greco-Roman history of the church.

We are now, perhaps, ready to conclude by returning to the question that has always been *the* question through all of this construction project. Assuming that most, if not all Christians, and many Jews as well, would in some manner, agree that "the Bible" and "the Word of God" are terms that belong together, *how* might this be so? It will be evident immediately that we are now using the language of faith and confession. No critical or historical investigation, however scientifically conducted, can verify that "the Bible" and "the Word of God" belong together. Yet all the historical work we have done has made it possible for us to return to the language of religious affirmation with a great deal more understanding and less naïveté. We will know better the implications of what we're confessing.

The Bible as the Church's Book and the Church as the Bible's People

The Bible contains stories of origin (or myth, if you prefer the anthropological term), heroic tales, folk wisdom, ancestral tables, prophetic exhortations, theological teachings, parables, liturgical songs, and prayers that have been a spiritual "home" for the people called Jews and Christians, and even to some extent, Muslims. These writings create, for those of us who hold them sacred, a "world" and a "culture" that provides us with a language for naming and appropriating our experiences. They bind us together in a community of shared values, beliefs, practices, and understandings. As we live in this "cultural home" that the Bible creates, we learn the "language" of the household and are able to make sense out of our lives and to orient ourselves in relation to the world around us, to other people and communities, and to that Ultimate Mystery we name God. It is the Bible that gives us the language for naming and describing who God is for us, and for determining how we can best live our finite human lives in a way that gives them meaning and purpose. There is a reciprocal relationship in which the human faith community produces the Bible (the historical processes we've studied), and the Bible, in turn, creates and shapes the community in its historical existence as it listens for the "Word of God."

Let me suggest a way to think about that process of listening for "the Word of God" in scripture that enables the faithful community to ground itself in the world in relation to God and to other human communities. To some extent, I will be oversimplifying what is a very complex reality, but for our purposes in this study it will serve as a reasonable starting point. In what follows, I will be directly speaking to my own tribe—the tribe of Christians. I am well aware that I will not be speaking *for* all Christians; the deep divisions within Christianity over how to understand and use the Bible are all too evident. I do hope that even those Christians who disagree with my approach or who feel a need to put the Bible's authority beyond all human questioning will nonetheless read on, if they haven't given up already. We may discover previously unknown areas of agreement. While my principal concern is for my own faith tradition, I hope that those of other faiths or no faith may also find it of interest or benefit in illuminating their own self-understandings.

"Word" is *dabar* in Hebrew; *logos* or *hrēma* in Greek. In many ancient (and some modern) cultures, ancient Semitic cultures among them, speaking was and is a performative act. The spoken word creates a new reality; it accomplishes something. This notion is especially character- istic of oral cultures. In the creation stories of Genesis, God speaks the "heavens and the earth" into being: "And God said, 'Be,' and it was so." In the story of Jacob and Esau competing for their father Isaac's bless- ing, modern readers often think, "What's the big deal? So he blessed the wrong son. He could have simply corrected himself and blessed the right one. After all, it was only words." But a word once spoken could not be called back, any more than a boxer can call back a punch once thrown. It performed what it said. Jacob, by deceit, got the blessing of the firstborn, and nothing could change that. A similar situation obtains in many parts of East Africa, where if a shaman curses someone, that person *is* cursed, and often sickens and dies. Even in our world, with a long history of lit- eracy and the scientific worldview, the spoken word still has the power to create or destroy. Think of how powerful are the words, "I love you," when spoken to a spouse or a lover or to a parent or child. Conversely, think how hurtful "you stupid idiot" may be. The old childhood rhyme, "Sticks and stones may break my bones, but words can never hurt me," is simply wrong. Words can wound and words can heal, as we all know. During World War II, sailors in the U.S. Navy grew very familiar with a slogan they saw posted in their barracks and around their naval bases. It was designed to enhance security: "Loose lips sink ships." If you spoke about things and the wrong ears heard it, there could be direct and dire consequences for you or your comrades.

Logos in Greek has some of the same "performative" connotations as the Hebrew *dabar*, but has more the sense of being a bearer of the speaker's own identity— an emanation or a "going forth" of the speaker. *Logos* is the presence of the speaker within the speech. It can also mean reason or rationality or revelation. For the Greeks, *logos* was the rational- ity perceived in the universe that held the universe together; the coher- ence of things is due to the divine *logos* or "word" which is nothing less than the presence of the Creator within the creation. "The Word became flesh," says St. John (John 1:14), in describing Jesus as the incarnation of the divine *logos*. Using another term, *hrēma*, which is often a synonym for *logos*, the writer of the Epistle to the Hebrews says of Christ, "He is the realization of God's glory and the exact imprint of God's very being, and he sustains all things by his powerful *word*."

Given these notions of "the word" in both the cultures and languages out of which the Bible came, I'd like to suggest a working understanding of the correspondence between "the Bible" and the phrase "the Word of God."

For Christians, the Bible is the primary and authoritative witness to the presence and activity of the Word of God in the world.

Let me unpack that a bit. We are aware that there is a whole spectrum or continuum of understandings within the Christian church about how the Bible and the phrase "the Word of God" belong together. Some "conservative" or "evangelical" Christians may equate the biblical text itself with "the Word of God," though some within those circles may hold a broader or more nuanced view. The Bible is sometimes referred to as "the Word of God written," or as "the infallible and inerrant Word of God." On the other end of the continuum, some "liberal" or "progressive" Christians may look at the Bible, if they look at it at all, as (at best) a "container" for the Word of God, a container full of stories, legends, myths, parables, sayings, songs, that constitute a record of individuals' and communities' reflections on their experiences of God. This record has to be carefully sorted through to find the "Word of God" hidden inside all the various other things (some of them quite terrible) one encounters in the Bible. Some on this end of the spectrum also hold more nuanced views, including some who are comfortable affirming a definite connection between "Bible" and "Word of God."

It is not necessary for us, for the purposes of this discussion, to locate ourselves at some point along that continuum. For now, we're trying to understand how we might speak of encountering the "Word of God" as we read the Bible. And for that purpose, it's important to realize that, as I said earlier, the Bible is the church's book and the church is the Bible's people. Christians are a people whose history and life has been shaped by the scriptures it inherited from ancient Israel and by those it produced itself. To say that, for Christians, the Bible is the primary witness to the presence and activity of the Word of God in the world, is to say something that is both objectively and historically true, in the sense that it is impossible to conceive of the Christian church as we know it apart from the Bible. If the early followers of Jesus had not had the scriptures of Israel to provide them with the worldview, interpretive clues and a religious language tradition for reflecting on their experiences with Jesus of Nazareth, no Christian church in the form that we know it could have emerged, and our New Testament could not have been written. The church itself is, in some sense, a scriptural creation. This is not to say that other factors were not also at work to create the church, but simply that the scriptures were an integral and indispensable factor in the church's emergence.

To say that the Bible is the authoritative witness is to make an affirmation of faith and a statement about our own understanding of who we are. We are *Christians*; that is, we belong to the global community that is the carrier of the long tradition of regarding this book as the sacred place where we discover how to identify and locate the *presence and activity of the Word of God in the world*. The church, by this relationship to the Bible, is continually formed and reformed by the Word that it hears. Christians seek to *understand* the Bible, not primarily from the perspective of disinterested scholarship, but from the position of *standing under* the Bible, as the *authoritative witness* to the Word of God. The sort of understanding that comes from disinterested scholarship can provide much useful information *about* the Bible, but it will never be the sort of understanding that has the power to transform individuals or communities. The sort of understanding that comes when an individual who is part of a group of people which has placed themselves under the authority of the scriptures and are committed to listening for the Word of God in their own concrete historical reality, is a transformed and transforming understanding. Such a "standing under" posture does not preclude the need for critical analysis of the Bible, using all the tools available to us. Rather, when all is said and done, all exegesis and eisegesis complete, all historical and cultural contexts identified to the best of our ability, "standing under" the scriptures is about our own decision to treat the Bible as having authority for our life, or more precisely, to consciously embed ourselves in the community that has, through two millennia, agreed to grant these writings normative authority for our life together. It is a posture of humility; it affirms that in these writings, we find our own personal and communal story illuminated, challenged, and provoked to action. Or as Lauren Winner puts it in her fine spiritual memoir *Still*, "it is life inside this Christian story that has begun to tell me who I really am."[1]

To say that the Bible is the primary and authoritative *witness to the presence and activity of the Word of God in the world* is to acknowledge that it did not simply drop out of heaven as a magical object, but is a collection of writings that grew out of the actual experiences of living human communities in their specific historical circumstances as they struggled to understand who they were, who God was, and what their

---

1. Lauren Winner, *Still*, 181.

relationship to God was. The "Word of God" is not synonymous with the text of the Bible. The Bible is a *witness* to the encounters with the Word of God by real people and communities. This delivers us from the fundamentalist or literalist absurdities of trying to explain away apparent errors or contradictions within the text of the Bible. We can deal with errors or contradictions in texts, even sacred texts, when we treat them, not as the thing itself (Word of God) but a witness to the thing itself as it has been encountered by real (fallible) people like us. No such thing as a perfect text can exist when all texts are produced by imperfect authors. The imperfections (contradictions, errors of fact, questionable theological judgments, bad translations, lost manuscripts, etc.) have been recognized and pondered and dealt with through centuries of careful, faithful, and honest interpretation by members of the faith community. This history of interpretation is the gift we inherit from past generations of our religious family, and it helps us in our own attempts to discern *the presence and activity of the Word of God in the world.*

This is not to say that biblical scholarship, with all its tools and skills at hand, should be neglected. But the use and value of what the scholar finds will, to a large extent, be controlled by his or her personal relation to the Bible. If the scholar stands above the text, looking at it from a position outside the living community of faith which produced, and has been produced, by that text, then the scholarship will have, at best, academic interest. But if the scholar stands under the text, as part of the community that confesses the authority of these texts for its grasp on its relation to the world and to other communities and to God, then the scholarship can be used to deepen the community's engagement with God and with the world at all levels.

It is also important, particularly for modern Western Christians, to remember that the Bible is the *church's* book. It is not the book of any individual. Individual interpretations of the Bible must always be checked against the interpretations of the other members of the community of faith, and of the larger community down through the ages. The church is the living community that has produced and been produced by the Bible. Since every individual Christian is embedded within that living community and is the carrier of that historical and reciprocal shaping process, the community is the matrix within which the task of listening for the Word of God must be undertaken if it is not to dissipate into chaos. The current firestorms within most major denominations, over the "hot button" issues we identified at the beginning of this study, could be dampened if partisans on both sides of those issues were willing to acknowledge that they cannot treat the Bible either as a weapon with which to vanquish the arguments of their opponents or as a hopelessly outdated, and therefore irrelevant, collection of texts that may be simply ignored in favor of contemporary cultural trends. The Holy Spirit does not reside in the text of the Bible. The Holy Spirit is given to the faithful community, and it is only as Christians engage one another in dialogue, careful listening, praying together, and a mutual "standing under" the Bible that the Bible can be legitimately and profitably used to illuminate the difficult questions of ours or any time.

To regard the Bible in this way means that the task of interpretation is not so simple as reading the Bible either "literally" or "metaphorically."[2] Care must be taken first to try to understand what the biblical writers were attempting to communicate in the particular culture, thought-world, and language of their own particular time and place in history. Any universal truth or "Word" must be extrapolated (exegesis is the technical name for this process) from the concrete historical, cultural, social, and linguistic particulars of a given text.

This task of interpretation has, in Christian circles, traditionally involved a three-sided interplay of Scripture, Tradition, and Reason. The eighteenth century Anglican priest John Wesley, founder of the movement known as Methodism, identified a fourth factor: Experience.

Scripture is always the primary, though not the exclusive witness to God's will and work in the world. St. Paul reminds us in Romans that the creation itself bears witness to God's existence and power, so there are other witnesses in addition to Scripture. But for the Christian community, Scripture functions as the primary witness because it contains the primal stories

2. I have great appreciation for Marcus Borg's efforts (*Reading the Bible Again*) to rejuvenate Christian faith for those who have given up on it for a variety of reasons, not least of which is the inability to accept the Bible as literally true or Jesus as anything other than a wise teacher. However, I could wish that he had found a more accurate and felicitous expression than to say that the Bible gives us "history metaphorized" (46ff). Quite apart from the fact that "metaphorized" is not a word, history cannot simply be read metaphorically. I understand that Borg is trying to convince people that it's all right not to believe that all stories in the Bible are factual reports of what happened. However, the opposite of "factual" or "historical" is not metaphor. More useful is his description of an older "natural literalism" versus a modern "conscious literalism" (8–9). The Bible contains history; it also contains folk tales, poems, liturgical material, stories of origin (myths), apocalyptic visions, miracle stories, etc. In all of these genres, metaphors may be present. The appropriate way to read any text depends on knowing what kind of text it is.

in which the faith community grounds its identity, and which bear witness to the community's encounters with God through time.

Tradition[3] is the accumulated wisdom, received interpretations, and customary practices of the larger faith community, guarded and transmitted *through time.* St. Paul, Justin Martyr, Origen, Augustine, Gregory of Nyssa, Francis of Assisi, Teresa of Avila, Lady Julian of Norwich, Martin Luther, John Calvin, John Wesley, Sojourner Truth, Dietrich Bonhoeffer, Dorothy Day, Pope John XXIII, and a whole host of other members of the Christian family through the ages are our conversation partners. There are many rabbinic interpreters from Judaism as well—Philo, Maimonides, Abraham Joshua Heschl, and others—who also contribute their own insights to the ongoing conversation with the Bible. Contemporary or individual interpretations of the Bible must always be checked against, and informed by, the interpretations of the other members of the whole community of faith.

Reason is, from a faith perspective, a God-given faculty and an essential aspect of our humanity. While faith may transcend reason, it cannot contradict it without violating something that makes us essentially who we are. Another way of saying this is that while truth cannot be reduced to rational*ism*, and may even, on occasion, be *supra*-rational, it cannot be (if it is really truth) *irrational.* Since humans are imperfect creatures, both by nature and by moral choice, human reason is sometimes flawed in its operations, and this reinforces the need for the other three elements in the process.

Experience is not merely personal, individual experience, but also the collective experience of the larger faith community borne out and made alive again in an individual's own experience. It is where the scriptural witness comes alive in mission and action in the particulars of the community's historical existence. Does a particular interpretation of scripture make a real difference in my life, in the life of the church, and in the world? Does the biblical word generate something within the community and its individual members that aligns the community's (and the individual's) actions with the direction of God's renewing and restoring work in the world?

To sum up, we could do worse than to answer the question "How good is the Good Book?" than by applying to the Bible Henry Wadsworth Longfellow's nursery rhyme that he composed for his infant daughter:

3. I like Jaroslav Pelikan's definition of tradition (*The Christian Tradition,* vol. 1, 6.): "Tradition is the living faith of the dead; traditionalism is the dead faith of the living."

> There was a little girl,
> Who had a little curl,
> Right in the middle of her forehead.
> When she was good,
> She was very good indeed,
> But when she was bad she was horrid. (Poem #835)

We've had no end of instances when "the Good Book" has been horrid because horridly used. The current "biblical wars" over the social issues we've identified, and all others as well, could become real conversations with mutual learning on both sides if partisans on both sides of those issues were willing to acknowledge that they "stand under" the authority of the scriptures, rather than over it, wielding it as a club to beat their opponents. But if we are willing to do the often difficult, sometimes painful, but always exhilarating work of engaging one another and the issues on the basis of our common commitment to the scriptures, we would allow the Word of God to which they bear witness to do its creating, liberating and transforming work. It is only as the faithful engage one another in dialogue, careful listening, praying together, and a mutually serious engagement with the church's scriptures that the Bible can be legitimately and profitably used to illuminate the difficult questions of ours or any time. Then "the Good Book" will prove itself, as it has through more than two millennia, to be "very good indeed."

Bibliography of Works Cited

"Anglican Bishops Condemn Homosexual Relations." No pages. Online: http://amarillo. com/stories/080798/new_LA0673.shtml.

Alter, Robert. *The Art of Biblical Narrative*. New York: Basic Books. 1981.

Aquinas, Thomas. *Summa Theologica*. II. II. 40.

Barton, John. *The Nature of Biblical Criticism*. Louisville: Westminster John Knox, 2007.

———. *Holy Writings, Sacred Text: The Canon in Early Christianity*. London: SPCK, 1997.

Bellah, Robert N. *Religion in Human Evolution: From the Paleolithic to the Axial Age*. Cambridge, MA: Belknap Press of Harvard University Press, 2011.

Borg, Marcus J. *Reading the Bible Again for the First Time: Taking the Bible Seriously But Not Literally*. San Francisco: HarperSanFrancisco, 2001.

Brueggemann, Walter. *Interpretation and Obedience: From Faithful Reading to Faithful Living*. Minneapolis: Fortress, 1991.

Carroll, James. *Constantine's Sword*. New York: Houghton Mifflin, 2002.

Childs, Brevard S. *Introduction to the Old Testament as Scripture*. Philadelphia: Fortress, 1979.

Cragg, Kenneth. *What Decided Christianity: Event and Experience in the New Testament*. Worthing, UK: Churchman, 1989.

Crossan, John Dominic. *Four Other Gospels: Shadows on the Contours of the Canon*. Minneapolis: Winston, 1985.

Drosnin, Michael. *The Bible Code*. New York: Touchstone, 1998.

Ehrman, Bart D. *Lost Christianities:The Battles for Scripture and the Faiths We Never Knew*. New York: Oxford University Press, 2003.

———. *Lost Scriptures: Books That Did Not Make It Into the New Testament*. New York: Oxford University Press, 2003.

———. *The New Testament: A Historical Introduction to the Early Christian Writings*. New York: Oxford University Press, 2000.

Fish, Stanley. "Intentions and the Canons of Legal Interpretation. " No pages. Online: http://opinionator.blogs.nytimes.com/2012/07/16/intention. and. the. canons. of. legal. interpretation/?hp.

Freedman, David Noel. "Canon of the OT." In *The Interpreter's Dictionary of the Bible*, Vol. Supplementary, edited by Keith Krim, Sr., et al., 130–36. Nashville: Abingdon, 1976.

Freeman, Charles. *A New History of Early Christianity*. New Haven, CT: Yale University Press, 2009.

Bibliography of Works Cited

Gagnon, Robert. "Why a New Translation of the Heidelberg Catechism Is Not Needed: And Why Homosexualist Forces in the PCUSA Seek It. " No pages. Online: http://www.robgagnon.net/articles/HeidelbergCatechismRetranslation.pdf.

Gamble, Harry Y. "Canon. New Testament." In *The Anchor Bible Dictionary, vol. I,* edited by David Noel Freedman, et al., 852–61. New York: Doubleday, 1992.

Gomes, Peter. *The Good Book: Reading the Bible with Mind and Heart.* New York: Harper Collins, 1996.

Hoyt, Herman A. *War: Four Christian Views.* Downer's Grove, IL: InterVarsity, 1981.

Jenkins, Philip. *Jesus Wars: How Four Patriarchs, Three Queens, and Two Emperors Decided What Christians Would Believe for the Next 1500 Years.* New York: Harper Collins, 2010.

Jenson, Robert. "The Father, He. . ." In *Speaking the Christian God: The Holy Trinity and the Challenge of Feminism,* edited by Alvin F. Kimmel, Jr., 95–109. Grand Rapids: Eerdmans, 1992.

Johnson, Luke Timothy. *Religious Experience in Earliest Christianity: A Missing Dimension in New Testament Studies.* Minneapolis: Fortress, 1998.

Kaufman, Gordon D. *In Face of Mystery: A Constructive Theology.* Cambridge, MA: Harvard University Press, 1993.

Kennedy, John W. "Patterson's Election Seals Conservative Control." *Christianity Today* (July 13, 1998) 21.

Kraft, Dina, and Laurie Goodstein. "Anglicans Face Wider Split Over Policy Toward Gays." No pages. Online: http://www.nytimes.com/2008/06/30/news/30iht.30anglican.14084545.html.

LaHaye, Tim, and Jerry B. Jenkins. *Left Behind: A Novel of Earth's Final Days.* Carol Stream, IL: Tyndale House, 1995.

Lord, Albert B. *The Singer of Tales.* Cambridge, MA: Harvard University Press, 1978.

Luther, Martin. *Preface to Revelation 1522.* Vol. 35. In *Luther's Works,* edited by Jaroslav Pelikan. St. Louis: Concordia, 1963.

Mack, Burton. *A Myth of Innocence: Mark and Christian Origins.* Philadelphia: Fortress, 1988.

Madigan, Kevin, and Jon Levenson. *Resurrection: The Power of God for Christians and Jews.* New Haven, CT: Yale University Press, 2008.

Meeks, Wayne. *The First Urban Christians.* New Haven, CT: Yale University Press, 1983.

Metzger, Bruce M. *The Canon of the New Testament: Its Origin, Development, and Significance.* Oxford: Clarendon, 1987.

Ong, Walter J. *The Presence of the Word: Some Prolegomena for Cultural and Religious History.* New Haven, CT: Yale University Press, 1967.

Pagels, Elaine. *Beyond Belief: The Secret Gospel of Thomas.* New York: Random House, 2003.

———. *The Gnostic Gospels.* New York: Random House, 1979.

———. *Revelations: Visions, Prophecy, and Politics in the Book of Revelation.* New York: Viking, 2012.

Pelikan, Jaroslav. *The Christian Tradition: A History of the Development of Doctrine, vol. 1.* Chicago: University of Chicago Press, 1971.

Ratzinger, Joseph (Pope Benedict XVI) and Adrian J. Walker. *Jesus of Nazareth Vol. 1: From the Baptism in the Jordan to the Transfiguration.* New York: Doubleday, 2007.

Rogers, Jack. *Jesus, the Bible, and Homosexuality.* Louisville: Westminster John Knox, 2006.

Rubenstein, Richard E. *When Jesus Became God: The Struggle to Define Christianity During the Last Days of Rome*. Orlando: Harcourt, 1999.

Sanders, James A. "Canon, Old Testament." In *The Anchor Bible Dictionary, vol. I*, edited by David Noel Freedman, et al., 847–52. New York: Doubleday. 1992.

Sawyer, John F. A. *The Fifth Gospel: Isaiah in the History of Christianity*. Cambridge, UK: Cambridge University Press, 1996.

Scanzoni, Letha, and Nancy Hardesty. *All We're Meant to Be: A Biblical Approach to Women's Liberation*. Waco, TX: Word, 1974.

Schneider, Sandra. *The Revelatory Text: Introduction to the New Testament as Sacred Scripture*. Collegeville, MN: St. John's, 1999.

Siker, Jeffrey. "Homosexuality, the Bible, and Gentile Inclusion." *Theology Today*, 51. No. 2 (July 1994) 219–34.

Smith, Wilfred Cantwell. *What Is Scripture? A Comparative Approach*. Minneapolis: Fortress, 1993.

Stammer, Larry B. "A Wife's Role is 'To Submit' Baptists Declare." No pages. Online: http://articles.latimes.com/1998/jun/10/news/mn. 58510.

Stendahl, Krister. "Qumran and Supercessionism: The Road Not Taken. " *The Princeton Seminary Bulletin*, 19:2 (1998) 134–42.

Sundberg, Jr., Albert C. "Canon of the New Testament. " In *The Interpreter's Dictionary of the Bible, Volume Supplemenatry,* edited by Keith Krim, et al., 130–36. Nashville: Abingdon, 1976.

Tillich, Paul. *Systematic Theology. Vol. 1*. Chicago: University of Chicago Press, 1973.

Watson, Francis. *Text, Church, and World: Biblical Interpretation in Theological Perspective*. Edinburgh: T & T Clark, 1994.

Winner, Lauren. *Still: Notes on a Mid-faith Crisis*. San Francisco: HarperOne, 2012.

www.ingramcontent.com/pod-product-compliance
Lightning Source LLC
Chambersburg PA
CBHW030850090426
42737CB00009B/1173